THE ART OF FLOWER ARRANGING

THE ART OF FLOWER ARRANGING

by Zibby Tozer

Introduction by Charlotte Ford

THE WARNER LIFESTYLE LIBRARY

WARNER BOOKS

A Warner Communications Company

THE WARNER LIFESTYLE LIBRARY

 Created by Media Projects Incorporated

Photography by Ed Rager
Illustrations by Gabriel Casuso
Glossary Illustrations by Zibby Tozer

Staff, Media Projects Incorporated
Carter Smith: President
Beverly Gary Kempton: Senior Editor
James E. Ramage: Designer
Ellen Coffey: Assistant Editor

Photographs:

Pages 26, 29, 30, 59, 73: Elvin McDonald
Page 57: Greg Komar, Inc.
Page 74: Courtesy of Jeanne Cameron Shanks

Warner Books, Inc., 666 Fifth Avenue, New York, N.Y. 10103

 A Warner Communications Company

Printed in the United States of America
First Printing: May 1981
10 9 8 7 6 5 4

Library of Congress Cataloguing in Publication Data

Tozer, Zibby.
The art of flower arranging.

(The Warner lifestyle library)
Includes index.
1. Flower arrangement. I. Title.
II. Series: Warner lifestyle library.
SB449.T69   745.92   80-21597
ISBN 0-446-51217-6 (hardcover)
ISBN 0-446-37945-X (pbk. U.S.A.)
ISBN 0-446-37946-8 (pbk. Canada)

Also in the Warner Lifestyle Library
The Art of Gift Wrapping
The Art of Table Decoration
The Art of Mixing Drinks

Contents

Introduction

I have always loved flowers, and not from afar. As a child I lived with them; as an adult I still do, and grow them also. Few things can soothe, please, and comfort as completely as flowers.

I am a great believer in putting them where they can be seen. If that seems an odd thing to say, think how often the glory of fresh flowers is confined to a dining room table which is used only sparingly. Or a living room, kept pristine because the family does not do its real living there. Instead, why not flowers in the foyer, the kitchen, the bathroom, the bedroom, those pillar posts of our existence? I do not buy a quantity of flowers or elaborate ones, unless I entertain or am celebrating a special event. But I *always* buy a few, and I have them in those rooms essential to me, namely my bedroom and on my bathroom sink where I can enjoy them every time I wash my face.

Many of us are intimidated by flowers—their cost, their care, the skills we imagine we must have to arrange them. True, flowers can be expensive, and designs intricate and time-consuming. But, in truth, flowers are far easier than they look and there is no reason to deny ourselves and others their beauty. With proper conditioning, which is quickly learned, flowers last longer; with some knowledge of tools and arranging materials, proportions, the idiosyncrasies of particular flowers, color, and the construction of basic arrangements, you can fashion whatever bouquet suits your fancy. And that could be regal one day, whimsical the next; sophisticated or ingenuous.

One of the delights of life today is the freedom we now have to express our various selves, in dress, the way we entertain, decorate our homes, and in our choice and use of flowers. Although I have an enduring fondness for white and purple lilies and flowers with a distinct aroma, my taste embraces just about all nature has to yield. In the summer I fill my home with varieties from my cutting garden; in the winter I often buy from a sidewalk stand to avoid the season's more inflated prices. And they can be avoided. Think daisies, for instance. I do, and use them all the time. Another ruse is a dinner table set with a single flower in a glass bud vase in front of each guest. It is intimate and enchanting, and better still means fewer flowers to buy and handle.

Mine are only a few thoughts. In *The Art of Flower Arranging* there are dozens more. Zibby Tozer knows flowers and knows how to help us be creative and practical. She even encourages a bit of duplicity with her instructions on how to fake a lily plant. She believes, as I do, in flowers all year long and all around the house. Here then are the tips, tricks and suggestions to make that possible, and splendid photographs to prove that it is. Force a bulb, fashion a twig wreath, dry some baby's breath. Arranging flowers satisfies the soul, and that, after all, is a reward of art.

Charlotte Ford

Charlotte Ford

1
The Basics

Quite simply, flowers are one of my greatest joys. Their scents always surprise me, and the vast spectrum of colors, shapes, textures, and sizes is a constant delight. Whenever I put together two dissimilar shapes of different colors and see them blend into one form, I have a sense of excitement.

Flowers can be a part of your daily life just as they are of mine. Despite tales to the contrary, they are not difficult to work with, and in this book I will describe how to do so with ease. Just as our choice of clothes and furniture expresses who we are and our uniqueness, so our choice and use of flowers do the same.

And living with them need not be expensive. True, cut flowers are not among today's bargains—little is—but some understanding of their particular characteristics will result in finer arrangements and less costly ones. A single bloom in a simple container, or a bunch of Queen Anne's lace picked in a field and set in an old teapot, for instance, is just as effective as the outsized and extravagant arrangement in an ornate vase. The lily need not be gilded.

Happily ours is a more accepting and casual age. No longer are we held fast by those strictures which dictated one, and only one, "proper" way to set a table, serve wine, or arrange flowers. Yes, even the display of flowers had its rules; and as history teaches us, rules spawn revolutionaries. It was in the 1940s that Judith Garden, legendary in the world of flowers, dared to offer her New York customers something other than the conventional arrangement of long-stemmed roses in a cylindrical vase. Her innovation, the loosely arrayed bouquet with the natural look of flowers freshly picked from the garden, is very much today's fashion.

There are times, however, when the occasion or the mood of the room makes a sculptural arrangement appropriate. The formal dining table bedecked with fine crystal hardly calls for a kitchen mold filled with daisies.

You do not have to be an artist to enjoy flowers, but as a painter I would like to share some thoughts that have affected the way I handle them. A wise teacher once explained that when molding clay on a potter's wheel the artist should remember that the pot and its glaze

Opposite: This wonderful flower arranger's cupboard is filled with the tools of the trade and a bounty of eclectic accessories.

must be in harmony. So too must flowers and their containers. A small glass perfume bottle is suitable for a single rose but not for a full-blown peony, as it would seem to be on the verge of toppling over even if it does not. The eye, then, is the teacher.

While a cutting garden is the best source for flowers and foliage, there are, of course, numerous florists with well-stocked refrigerators of seasonal and unusual flowers. And do not overlook that inexhaustible source, fields with their abundance of wildflowers. Wherever you find them, there cannot be too many flowers and flowering plants in your home. Create a spirited atmosphere of discovery with a variety of them—delicate nosegays in squat containers, a sumptuous flowering plant in a pretty basket, miniature lady apples in a small bowl, forsythia branches in tall vases. Add life to every room in your house, and avoid that static and dreariest use of flowers, endless formal arrangements, all of which seem conceived by strangers rather than those who live there.

Flower arranging and styling can be taught and learned. Taste cannot be taught, but with a sensitive and interested eye it can be learned. Study nature, that wondrous repository of symmetry, style, and the drama of change. But most of all, to achieve style with flowers, please yourself first. If you are happy with your arrangement, it is a success.

Basic Tools and Supplies

There are a few basic tools that are helpful and necessary when working with flowers. Most can be found in the housewares section of any large department store.

A good knife is indispensable. The typical florist's knife is a jack-knife with a dull point at the end of the blade. However, any sharp knife will do, including a kitchen knife.

Flower stems should always be cut with a knife, never scissors — not even shears — as they crush the cells through which the stem draws water. But you will need shears to cut heavy, woody flower stems, branches, autumn foliage, rhododendrons, etc. (I admit that, for convenience, I use scissors when cutting flowers in the garden, and then recut with a knife as I arrange them.)

The aids for holding flowers in their containers are numerous. The most popular are bricks of plastic foam (known as green foam) and metal-weighted "frogs," which tend to be costly and not always easy to come by. Frogs are fashioned in myriad sizes and shapes and are commonly referred to as pinholders, although one variation does not have sharp pinpoints but a latticework top in addition to the cage enclosing its base. (It is also made in glass and plastic, but the sturdier metal version is preferable.) This one is harder to work with than the pinholder, but is useful with arrangements of heavy-stemmed flowers, or branches. Pinholders can be held fast in containers with waterproof tape; however, I prefer not to do so as it makes washing difficult, and clean containers are vital to flowers' freshness.

Green foam, which comes in many densities, is a quick and tractable tool. The very dense foam must be soaked for two hours before using. That of lighter density needs only minutes to absorb water; however, it tends to crumble and can seldom be used a second time. (Instead of storing green foam on a shelf, where it will dry out between uses, I keep it in a small bucket of water.)

Using a knife, cut the foam to fit your container. If it is transparent, such as clear glass, galax leaves or any other pretty leaves make a handsome camouflage. Place the leaves flat against all sides of the container, and the inelegant foam will be elegantly hidden. Extend the foam a good inch or more above the top of the container, to enable you to angle your greens and flowers over the edge. Unless the foam is cut to the precise shape of the bowl, you might want to secure it. Crisscross a few strips of waterproof or paraffin tape from one edge of the bowl over the foam to the opposite edge. And if it needs to be fortified further, run the tape around the bowl's entire top rim. Most trades evolve their own idiom, and flower arranging is no different. We call the waterproof and paraffin tape we use so often "stickum," not a word of refinement, but a descriptive one which any florist will recognize if you wish to buy rolls of it.

It is important that the foam be thoroughly wet, and given water every few days to keep it moist. Otherwise, it will draw water from the stems of the flowers and shorten their lives. To make a very high arrangement in a tall vase, place extra pieces of foam in the bottom of the vase to support the top piece into which the flowers are inserted.

A third helpful device, particularly with a very full arrangement, is a web of chicken wire which you can cut to the shape of your container. Although it is more durable than foam, it does tend to rust in water. I often secure it with stickum to the upper part of the container, where it will not be completely immersed.

There are only two essentials of flower arranging, a sharp knife and a vase, but for the well-equipped cupboard, I would suggest the following:

Containers of various sizes
A sharp knife
Scissors and/or shears
Pinholders of various sizes
Green foam
Chicken wire
Medium-gauge floral wire
   (Some flowers need to be wired for strength. I use 22-gauge green
      wire.)
Baskets and liners
   (Plastic food containers from the market or delicatessen are
      good.)

Buckets
  (Tall and short ones.)
Natural charcoal
Cut-flower food
Floral tape
  (Waterproof tape and paraffin tape.)
Floral stem-wrapping tape
  (Green or brown non-sticky tape available at most florists.)
Plastic watering can
  (One with a long, narrow spout allows you to water arrangements without disturbing the flowers.)
Plastic spray bottle
  (It is helpful in misting flowers, to prevent too much water loss through transpiration.)
Sphagnum moss
Flower vials
  (Also known as aqua picks, these are small plastic tubes sealed with tight-fitting rubber caps with a hole in each. The vial is filled with water and the flower stem poked through the cap's hole.)

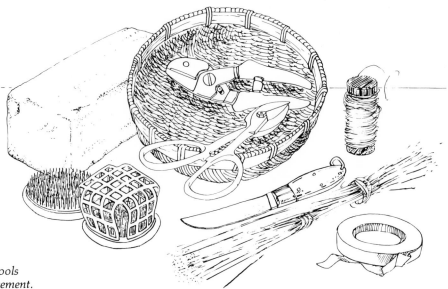

A collection of the basic tools needed to make an arrangement.

Conditioning

When you pick flowers from the garden, you know they are fresh. When selecting them at the florist's, look for blooms with petals facing up toward the flower center. This signals their freshness. Reject those with centers that have advanced to the "seed" stage, and with leaves and stems that seem tired. Some flower heads, however, stay fresh even after their outer leaves have withered. Chrysanthemum leaves, for instance, shrivel and dry up several days before the head of the flower wilts. Simply remove the unsightly leaves and let the flower live on.

The most important lesson to be learned in conditioning flowers is to cut their stems with a knife and put them in lukewarm water as soon as possible. It is an amazing fact, often with sad results, that in a matter of minutes the water-drawing capillaries at the base of the stem close up, and the glorious bouquet you just bought may be choked of all its vibrance.

Flowers from the garden should be picked at that point neither too early nor too late in their cycle. If gathered prematurely, the bud's development comes to an abrupt halt; if picked too late, the blossom dies too early. Tree branches should be cut when the buds are tight, as the warmth of the house helps them open nicely.

Try to pick flowers early in the day, when they have had a long cool night to regain strength from the previous day's warmth. The end of the day is also good, but avoid midday, when they lose too much of their moisture to the air. Have a bucket of lukewarm water on hand, and put the cut flowers in it immediately. Lukewarm or room temperature water should be used because a flower's capillaries draw it more quickly than hot water, which can wilt the flower or stem, or cold water, which can shock it. Many of the instructions for the proper conditioning of flowers are based on the fundamentals of capillary action.

Whether you have bought flowers or picked your own, they will last longer if you follow a few elementary rules.

Depending on the arrangement, stems can be cut a little or a lot but, again with that knife I keep brandishing, cut them at an angle to expose the maximum number of cells on the new surface of the stem. A diagonal cut also produces a point, which in turn prevents

Cutting a flower the right way is important. With the flower head away from you, cut a definite diagonal slice with a knife.

the stem from resting flat on the bottom of the container, blocked from its access to water. Cut flowers just under the leaf node, their nutrient storage pocket. The stems of fibrous-stemmed flowers, such as asters, stock, and chrysanthemums, need more cells exposed to water than other flowers do. Break the stems, slit them with a knife two or three inches from the end, and lightly scrape them at the base. Take the time to scrape daisies too; it prolongs their life even further.

The second step in the cleaning process is the removal of much of the foliage, especially foliage below the waterline, as it rots easily and pollutes the water with bacteria which attack and clog flower stems. Next, strip the bulk of the remaining leaves from the stem. Water is drawn upward, and the idea is to thwart its passage to the leaves first and clear the path to the flower head. This is particularly important for daisies and roses; the latter should also have the thorns below the waterline removed. As long as flowers have a fresh supply of water, they keep their freshness.

When the stems are cut or broken, place the flowers loosely in a bucket of lukewarm water in a dark spot for an hour or more before arranging. Overnight is even better. If you feel your flowers look naked after all this surgery, do not shy from a bit of fakery when arranging them. Add some of the more attractive pieces of cut foliage to the vase. Even your best friend will not know.

Once the flowers are properly groomed and in place, they still need attention — or, more accurately, the water does. There are many remedies to rid water of the bacteria "hatched" by the normal rotting process of flower stems, and it is important to do so, as bacteria shorten a flower's life by 50 percent. The most effective means is a small nugget of natural charcoal — wood charcoal is good — at the bottom of the container. The small charcoal bricks used for outdoor cooking are not suitable, because they are chemically treated. I am also partial to flower food, and add whatever amount is called for in the directions. It corrects the water's acid-alkali balance, inhibits the growth of bacteria, and provides nutrients normally generated by the plant roots. Save aspirin for human life; with plants it causes mischief. Pennies, on the other hand, do not. Tulips, for example, respond well to the chemical properties of copper pennies. Today, unhappily, this is more fiction than fact, as pennies are merely copper plated.

When all is said and done, the best way to keep flowers lively is to remove them, clean the container, and fill it again with plenty of fresh lukewarm water. Rinse the part of each stem that has been below the waterline, recut them, and plunge the flowers into clean water. If you do not have time for this, just add fresh water to your flowers daily.

Bulb flowers, such as narcissus, iris, and hyacinth, have a film inside their stems which oozes a thick sap, or latex, and must be washed off to leave the stem clear to draw water. Also, most bulb flowers, once cut, have a white tip at their ends which should be snipped off, again to clear the stem. (Woody flowers are helped if their ends are lightly hammered.) Tulips, too, "bleed" after they are cut. To stop the flow of sap, try singeing the stems with a match.

One cautionary note. Do keep flowers away from heat — sunny windows, under lamps, warm fireplaces — which causes their petals to lose moisture.

These, then, are the general steps for conditioning flowers. Certain flowers have particular conditioning needs, and those you will find described in the appendix.

Containers and Proportions

Containers are all about you. Seek and ye shall find. In the kitchen, the china closet, the storeroom. Copper molds, ceramic molds, casserole dishes, sugar bowls, pitchers, drinking glasses, sauceboats, apples, pumpkins—all make lovely and unusual containers. So too do old perfume bottles, wooden tea caddies, baskets, baked bean crocks, cookie tins, and silver serving bowls. The possibilities are as vast as your imagination. If you have flowers throughout your home—and I hope you do—try to have on hand containers of varying shapes and sizes: large, small, clear, opaque, some for masses of flowers, some for a single flower. And do not overlook the versatile plastic food container. It is an excellent liner and can transform a non-water-retaining vessel—a basket or a tea caddy—into a stunning container.

Much of your flowers' life depends on the care you give their containers. Clean, clean, clean is the message. The bacteria that naturally form in the water cling to the sides of the vases and cannot be removed simply by washing with soap. Use ammonia or white vinegar; both are solvents. When a transparent vase looks cloudy, it is a sign of bacterial scum. Clean it thoroughly before using it again. Do the same with all equipment, especially your cutting tools, to keep them free of bacteria.

Some rules are made to be broken, and what pleasure there is in doing so. Such are the rules of scale and proportion. But do not get too carried away. Distortion can end with high drama or misfortune. The shape of the container you use provides a preliminary guide to the shape of the arrangement—a round arrangement in a round bowl, an oblong display in an oblong container.

A basic rule of thumb is that an arrangement be two-and-one-half times the size of its container. This is not carved in stone, however, and a delicate vase might be in truer harmony with an arrangement only twice its size, while a heavy sculptural pot needs a large array of flowers with a weighty look. Tall, wispy flowers or short, dainty ones are correct for a container that looks light. A mass of heavy-headed mums is not. When the proportions are right, the flowers will look natural.

The heavy-headed orchid branches are proportionally correct in their squat containers, a 19th-century Chinese pot and a glass ginger jar filled with black rocks.

The airy freesia looks right in the light glass cylinder, while the small Chemex beaker is a perfect bud vase for the stalk of miniature carnations.

Once your arrangement and its vase are in tune, study your room for that spot where the display will be most in accord with its surroundings. Generally, an arrangement for a side table already filled with other objects should be light and airy. The array for a buffet table, on the other hand, can be on the grand scale, and, indeed, bold arrangements are quite luxurious on such a table. The scale of a basket of reeds and a profusion of cattails would complete an elegant yet casual buffet supper setting.

A second rule of thumb calls for dinner table arrangements 13 to 15 inches high. A clever way to test the height of your arrangement as you make it is the elbow-to-clenched-fist method. In this one instance, firmly rest your elbow on the table and clench your fist. If the flowers are taller than the top of your fist, your dinner guests will not be able to see one another across the table. Moreover, the total arrangement might seem too large in scale for the table. An alternative to the traditional 13- to 15-inch arrangement is to think tall—flower heads well above the normal eye level of your seated guests. An amaryllis plant, as an example, is a splendid centerpiece. The slender stalk allows diners to see each other, and thus does not inhibit conversation as will a dense arrangement at eye level. I often use clusters of different bud vases on my dinner table and place a single tall flower in each to set a particularly convivial mood. Or, for a touch of the theatrical, parade a row of crocks filled with open forsythia branches down a long dinner table.

Color

The thought of color need not trigger an anxiety attack. In all honesty, the colors I use are dictated more by my moods than my theories. Allow yourself the same freedom. There are no set color rules. I find it pleasing to use flowers of the same color family together; however, this too can be misleading. Cornflower blue somehow does not work well with some shades of purple, and an orangy pink generally quarrels with a rosy one.

Colors are best understood by looking at the color wheel. The three basic colors are red, yellow and blue, and all—yes, *all*—

Opposite: A pair of monochromatic flower arrangements illustrates the many hues of white.

colors are made up of a combination of these. White and black are not valued in the color wheel. Their major function is to give colors tonal value, a feeling of weight or depth.

The notion of temperature in color should not be overlooked. Yellows and reds are warm colors; blues and greens are cool. Knowledgeable restaurateurs always decorate with warm colors, usually in the orange-red family. In hot climates, however, decorating with cool colors is more popular.

Hue refers to a particular shade or tint. Value is the relative lightness or darkness of a color, and is indicated by the amount of white or black used to make the color. A darker color is called a shade of the original color, while a lighter color is a tint. Intensity, in the color vocabulary, refers to a color's strength or weakness. Neutral colors are weak in hue — light beige or dark gray-green. To the eye, a strong yellow leaps forward. Blue, on the other hand, recedes, and for that reason I never recommend using blue flowers at night or for a wedding. The pale blue delphinium may be a most glorious flower, but in the evening it is nearly impossible to detect in a dimly lit room.

The shades and tints of blues, reds, oranges, greens, purples, and even of whites and blacks, are infinite. Indeed, many of the modern painters who emerged from the WPA's Federal Art Project stunned the world in the 1930s and '40s with their all-white and all-black works, which demonstrated the exciting range of these "valueless" colors. Take a close look at the petals of a daisy — they are really pink-white — or a spider mum, whose petals are green-white, or stephanotis, the bridal blossom, which is cream-white. Actually, the black eye of a black-eyed Susan is brown-black with a purple cast.

An interesting use of color is a monochromatic arrangement, technically flowers of one color. In fact, such arrangements consist of flowers of all one *hue*. When driving through the country, my daughters and I often play a game of finding just how many different greens exist. I cannot tell you the precise number, but nature's plethora of greens keeps us going for miles. Indeed, for an alternative to flowers, an exciting arrangement can be made simply of foliage. Combine different colors of green, different shades of the same green, and an assortment of shapes and textures.

Basic Flower Arrangement

When selecting flowers for an arrangement, consider the shapes of the heads of the flowers and look for those that blend with one another. Look too at textures, a variety of which adds character. Again, the rules are for breaking. Create a new shape by closely clustering little flower heads, and a new color by the interaction of two flower colors placed snugly together. On the whole, a rule which holds true is the one about weight. Large heavy blossoms are best kept low in a display; light, lyrical, or airy blossoms are especially pleasing on the perimeters of an arrangement. Beware of the commercial florist who uses one heavy mum at the top of a grouping. He has broken the rule unsuccessfully by vexing the eye, which is conditioned to the idea of gravity.

The most common arrangement, and the basic one, is the "mass" arrangement. Once you have mastered its techniques, and they are not awesome, you will be able to fashion bouquets for any occasion.

1. Select your flowers. For this arrangement, I used gerbera and marguerites (also known respectively as African daisies and white daisies), tuberoses, and leather leaf.

Assemble your equipment. For those new to the art, work with green foam, the easiest of the flower arrangers. Pictured are: green tape, green foam, scissors suitable for snipping wire, a glass liner, a basket, and a sharp knife.

2. Cut the thoroughly wet foam to fit the glass liner. Crisscross green tape over the foam, and secure it by running a strip of green tape around the edge of the liner.

3. The next step is the greening of the arrangement, which can be done after the flowers are in place, but is less awkward if handled first. Essentially, greens are used to cover the foam, and are not esthetically vital to the arrangement. Keep them short; you can always add longer pieces later. In this case, I used leather leaf fern — a hardy one which holds up well — cut it, and stuck it in the foam. When the foam is blanketed, the greening is complete.

4. You are now ready to place the first flower. (Number 1 in the diagram.) The height of that flower determines the overall size of the entire arrangement. Following the trusty rule of thumb, I cut the gerbera stem and placed it in the middle of the foam so that the height of the flower, plus its foam base, is approximately two-and-one-half times that of the basket.

5. Next, form the perimeter by putting the two lowest flowers in the foam (Number 2 in the diagram), or four flowers if the arrangement is to be round and seen from four sides. Here, the peach gerbera define the basic width of the arrangement.

6. Mold the arrangement's form with more flowers (Number 3 in the diagram), making them shorter than the tallest flower.

7. The two flowers in the front of the arrangement are now put into place. (Number 4 in the diagram.) The red gerbera is set rather low, to cover a portion of the front of the basket.

8. Once the perimeters of the arrangement are defined, a house of flowers is effortless. The gentle tuberoses and daises are fixed at random, filling in the gaps and spaces created by the gerbera. To give the arrangement depth, some flower stems are cut rather short at this point, and sunk deep into the foam. As more flowers are added, the arrangement gains density. Remember to angle the flowers for a natural look.

9. The only flower heads to extend further than the gerbera are a few very feathery blossoms, which do not detract from the arrangement's basic shape.

Now stand back and enjoy the magic you have worked. Keep it at its best as long as possible by adding water often. Whenever you can, tip the entire arrangement over the sink, pour out the old water, and fill with fresh water.

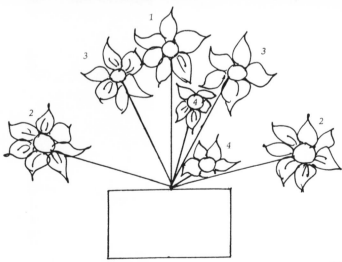

Different Moods

Flowers on the dinner table tell your family and guests that they were expected and you are happy they are there. With your choice of flowers, tablecloth or mats, china, glassware, and candles, you create the mood for the evening.

A. This informal setting, with its flavor of a French country house, is as inviting as the elegant formal table dressed for guests in black tie and long gowns. The flowers' container is, as it should be, a woven basket of clay. (Remember not to make the arrangement higher than eye level — 13″ to 15″ high — or the guests might be inclined to remove it and subvert your design.) The flowers too are as they should be — marigolds, daisies, white tuberoses, and chincherinchees befitting the china and napkins, actually French dish cloths. All speak with a casual voice.

B. Same table, same china, but the spirit changes with the flowers. Individual glass bottles of Queen Anne's lace, that ever-hardy weed, lend it a capricious air. Keep the heavy flower heads above or below eye level.

A. A formal table with flowers in individual vases, decorated with strands of raffia. Although some of the glass containers are of better quality than others, on the table they blend for a festive air. The tall bluish-purple blossoms are agapanthus, the tall pink ones, nerines; the peach-colored roses are sonia roses, while the orange flowers are miniature hybrid carnations and gerbera. Scattered about are wildflowers.

B. Again, only the flowers have been changed. Elegance and excitement are achieved by flanking each place card with a tiny full-blown sonia rose in a glass basket, and a single votive candle in a frosted glass. Bare birch branches, yellow and white lilies, nerines, gerbera, roses and agapanthus are held in the centerpiece container, actually a mushroom basket from the supermarket transformed into a mossed log by my 12-year-old daughter, who tied pieces of moss to it with thin spool wire. She and I then tied water-filled vials (aqua picks) of the various flowers to the branches with brown floral tape, and put them in a dry brick of green foam in the basket. (The branches do not need to absorb moisture from the foam.) I masked the green foam with moss and loose excelsior — shredded packing material — and made certain the densest part of the arrangement was below eye level. It took time to make, but what a dazzling sight it was!

2
Spring

Bulbs
and Branches

Spring. Celebrated spring, a time of awakening, abundance, and color. In many ways, it is the most exciting of all the flower seasons.

The slow renaissance of springtime beauties means such lovely bulb flowers as the crocus, the daffodil, tulip, hyacinth, and iris; those grand blooming branches of dogwood, forsythia, cherry, plum, and flowering magnolia; and the splendor of such flowering plants as the cineraria and azalea.

Spring bulbs lend themselves to any number of arrangements. Take an oversized terra-cotta saucer and fill it with bulbs in bloom. They can be bulbs of the same type, or a mixture of varieties, as long as their different heights are in unison.

Bulb arrangements are among the simplest to compose. Fill the bottom of a saucer with dirt or sand. One by one, place each bulb, including its roots, in the saucer, and spread the roots over the dirt. (Large saucers have sides high enough to offer bulbs the support they need to keep them from tipping over.) With your fingers, push extra dirt between the bulbs, but leave the top half of each bulb exposed. Quite apart from the flowers and leaves, the bulbs themselves are visually intriguing, some would even say beautiful. Add a finishing touch with a sprinkle of tiny white and yellow pebbles, or polished gray stones, over the dirt. Pebbles are particularly pretty with narcissus and hyacinth bulbs; oddly, I prefer a moss cover with tulip bulbs. Most florists and garden supply houses, by the way, stock these adornments.

If you use moss, do so correctly. Whether it is picked in the forest or bought at the florist, the treatment is the same. Moss should be kept slightly damp in a heavy plastic airtight bag. When you are ready to use it, soak the amount you need in a bucket, then tear it into pieces as soon as it has absorbed water. Use extra force as you press it in the dirt. When your plant has passed its prime, remove the moss and return it to its storage bag. One precaution: When watering a plant with a moss blanket, remember to soak it adequately to be certain the roots receive water, not just the moss.

Opposite: A canal of grape hyacinths in Holland's Keukenhof Gardens is flanked by beds of tulips.

A single bulb in a terra-cotta bowl or traditional flowerpot is most attractive with moss around it. Or, for a lovely effect, you might group single bulbs of different types, each in its own pot. I often use a flat basket to hold a cluster of individual bulb pots with moss in them. But a lone bulb in a miniature clay pot on a miniature saucer will stand tall and spritely, and enhance any desk top.

As clay is not absorbent, protect your tabletops from damage with saucers under all clay flowerpots and bowls. For a one-night stand — a party, perhaps — you can do without a saucer for a bowl, but do keep one under a flowerpot to make it look natural. A potted geranium as a centerpiece is charming, but minus its customary saucer the poor pot looks embarrassingly undressed, indeed, stark naked.

The simple is often the most classic. If that appeals to you, put bulbs in clear glass containers filled with stones and a small amount of water. The sparkle of clear glass makes it a marvelous material to use at any time; and the glass need not be cut crystal. A straight-sided glass casserole is a perfectly fine container for a bulb arrangement. Fill it with enough water to cover the bottom portion of the bulbs, and enough stones to keep the bulbs erect. Angled bulb flowers seem unnatural, because we are accustomed to seeing them grow upright in the garden.

Narcissus bulbs, especially when in bloom, may give off a delicious aroma, but their long slender leaves and narrow stalks tend to fall over. One solution is to loosely tie a strand of raffia around the middle of the narcissus plant. (A good source for raffia is an old Japanese mat. If you happen to have one, just cut it apart.)

In all probability the bulbs you buy from a florist will have been forced. They tend to produce weaker-stemmed flowers, and cannot be forced again. However, if they are planted outdoors they will bear flowers in their second year, and then annually.

Do not belittle the branch. Branches are spectacular, and they are fashionable. Not only do a few graceful branches suggest size and abundance, but the blossoms on cut branches have a long life.

Opposite: Paper-white narcissus fill a pretty porcelain bowl.

Left: Forsythia branches and ranunculi are exciting signs of spring. Right: Dogwood branches are beautiful next to pots of vanda orchids.

After buying or cutting your branches, pound them with a hammer so they will draw water. Remove an inch or two of the bottom bark and stand them in deep water. Change the water after five days or so. If the branches have buds, you will have the fun of watching them develop indoors. Tight buds benefit from misting; the shower technique works as well. Once, in my eagerness to force buds, I placed several branches in a bucket in the bathtub, away from the warm shower water. After a few hours of exposure to the lukewarm mist, the buds popped open.

Tulips

With spring come those wondrous old favorites—lilies, wildflowers, orchids, peonies, lilacs, and, of course, tulips. Known for some one thousand years, the tulip began life in the East. A Persian legend tells us that the first tulips sprang from drops of blood shed by a lover; thus the tulip came to signify devotion. Such was its magnetism that the Ottoman Empire used it as a symbol. And in the 1600s, Holland, the center of tulip culture, was seized by tulipomania—a period of wild speculation when single tulip bulbs commanded prices equivalent to several thousand dollars. Continuing its march across the world and through history, the tulip captured the imagination of the English, who celebrated a golden age of tulips in the mid-1800s, and the fantasies of the Pennsylvania Dutch, who used it so frequently in the designs of their pottery that today it is called tulip ware.

Tulips are among the few flowers that actually grow, once cut and placed in water. They also move and flop, creating their own natural scheme and, perhaps to your dismay, changing your concept of how they should be grouped. In short, they seem to have minds of their own.

As much as I like to mix tulips with other flowers, I particularly love them alone. A short glass cylinder filled simply with tulips of the same color is radiant.

Tulips need special care in the conditioning stage. Wrap them in strong, non-absorbent paper, such as waxed paper, and tape or staple the paper to keep the column sturdy. Cut the tulip stems with a knife an inch or more from the base, and put the bundle in a bucket of lukewarm water. (Never stand them in hot water, or their stems will collapse.) By drawing water, the tulips will become "hardened" while in a vertical position. Tulips need this conditioning because they are transported from the grower to the wholesaler, or florist, in large boxes which are so tightly packed with wrapped bunches that the flowers are quite bent. Proper conditioning does not always produce an erect tulip, but it prevents one from doubling over completely.

An extra tip: Remove the bottom tulip leaf, and check the base of the stem to see that it is clean. Often soil is trapped between the crevices where the leaf and stem join, and will cloud the water and hasten the flower's demise.

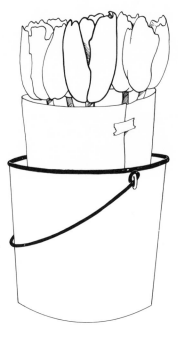

The tulips are supported by a tube of non-absorbent paper, to straighten their stems.

My grandmother's favorite Victorian trumpet vase is especially charming filled with a bouquet of peonies.

Peonies

To the ancient Chinese, the peony was the "King of Flowers," a badge of wealth and nobility, and a bearer of good fortune. It is more of spring's largesse. Peonies are effective en masse, or with lilac branches. Peonies can also be successfully mixed with other flowers; however, as they are heavy-headed, they are best placed low, close to the neck of the container. Try peonies with roses, a beautiful combination. Cut or buy peonies in the bud stage, and condition them as you would other flowers. The blossoms should open after a day in lukewarm water. If patience is not one of your virtues, a few hours in very hot water will produce flowers, but it is a risky practice, as it abbreviates their life. Do not forget the trick of removing most of the lower foliage and using the best leaf stalks to add fullness to the arrangement. They seldom need foliage, as their own is so attractive. Peonies can be irritating. I am often cross with them for not knowing their place, and moving about in the arrangement. The weight of those grand open blossoms bends the stem a bit, sometimes enough to make it necessary to rework the arrangement. In the garden, full-blown peonies tend to flop over and look messy. The English tidy things up by driving sticks into the peony bed and lashing the underdeveloped buds to them. When the peonies are in blossom, the foliage camouflages the sticks and the eye encounters a seemly and proper garden. Unfortunately, the peony season is rather short — early May to mid-June. By the way, for unknown reasons, the vibrant dark pink peony is called red. Similarly, the dark pink azalea is also "red." Mystifying, but so be it.

Wildflowers

A luxury of country living is the abundance of wildflowers, whether in a nearby field or outside your back door. By all means, bring them inside, and, if you wish, mix them with garden flowers, grasses, and herbs. But heed their style and keep them casual, in arrangements that are not fussed over, and never pretentious. Contain them in a crock, a basket, or any other vessel with a rustic air.

Despite the name, wildflowers are no less cultivated than their kin from nurseries and tended gardens. "Cultivated" simply denotes flowers transported from the part of the world to which they are indigenous to another part. Florida's weed can become New York's most cultivated and treasured houseplant.

An important tip: Pack flowers loosely in containers, thus allowing room for oxygen to reach the water and feed the flowers. I mention this here because, when arranging wildflowers particularly, there is a great temptation to stuff a crock with them. They might look as glorious as they do in the open field, but they could be choking.

Wildflowers are fragile, and need gentle care. They should be cut in the early morning, when their stems have absorbed the night's moisture. To protect the species, never pluck wildflowers,

as there is too great a danger of pulling up the roots. Slip them into a pail of water as soon as possible, or tie them tightly in a plastic bag with some wet moss in it. They can then be conditioned in the normal fashion.

A final note of caution: As many wildflowers are endangered, the field where they are found should never be totally stripped.

Lilies

Easter and Passover are two of spring's most noble festivals, and the Easter lily one of the season's most princely flowers. In fact, the Easter lily is only one member of the lily family, albeit the hardiest, and sweet smelling too. Although we think of lilies as white — for centuries the lily has denoted purity — they actually grow in every color except blue. In this country the most common lilies are the auratum (white and somewhat speckled), the pink and white rubrum, the orange lily, yellow lily, and white lily. The auratum, which should only be considered in moments of extravagance, has a heavenly scent, and is often used in formal weddings. The rubrum lily is the queen, and vies with anemones, tulips, and peonies as the most popular flower. Everyone, it seems, loves rubrum lilies. Their color is appealing, white speckled with rosy pink, and their shape is extraordinary. The elegant branchlike formation of the stalk gives the rubrum a large yet light and buoyant scale. Let them reign in solitary splendor, or mix them in arrangements. A single rubrum stem in a narrow clear glass vase is seldom inappropriate. The orange lilies at the florists are called mid-century lilies, and are often confused with the paler orange day lily and the deep orange tiger lily commonly seen in gardens. The mid-century lily is long lasting, while the bloom of the day lily survives, as its name indicates, only a day. Yellow lilies and red ones, though available, are usually imported and costly. Alstroemeria — also called Peruvian lily — ixia, and agapanthus, often identified as lilies, are actually not part of the *Lilium* genus.

Opposite: A glorious bouquet of wildflowers in an antique milk pail sits on the steps of a New York townhouse to welcome guests for a Sunday brunch.

Rubrum lilies, Easter lilies, and three other species of the genus Lilium *are combined in one grand bouquet.*

Lily bulbs bloom only once a year, and consist of scales bare of the protective jackets that encase tulip and narcissus bulbs. Consequently, they must be kept covered to protect them from drying out.

Here are some pointers on dealing with lilies: Scrape the heavy-stemmed varieties as soon as the buds open, and remove their anthers (pollen sacs) to slow down the opening of the flower and prevent the pollen from falling and staining. A failing of this virtuous flower is that its pollen stains everything from your hands to its own petals. If your lilies, particularly rubrums, are not as open as you might like, pry back the petals of an almost open bud with your fingers or tweezers. As the stalk draws water, the bud will continue to open.

Orchids

Most varieties of lilies are lasting and expensive, but not as hardy or as costly as orchids. Nonetheless, orchids are popular. Those most in demand today are the cymbidium, and such delicate branches of tiny orchids as the dendrobium and the oncidium. A lovely gift is a branch of cymbidium, which can live up to three weeks in a vase of water, or a single cymbidium orchid. A lady can wear it in her hair for an evening and never fear that it might wilt.

A few branches of tiny orchids in small Chemex beakers are always enchanting, but remember they are not nearly as robust as the cymbidiums. Keep the small scale of the flowers in mind, too, and give them a simple background. These lacy orchids are lost in a busy, patterned room.

There are endless tricks in our trade. One is to weight a heavy cymbidium branch, which could tip over your vase, with a handful of smooth black stones. They are handsome and can be used time and again — to adorn the dirt of the plant in a terra-cotta pot, for instance.

Orchid branches of the genus Phalaenopsis *and galax leaves in green foam make an arrangement that simulates a living plant.*

3
Summer

After the opulent flowers of spring and their equally opulent prices, summer is a welcome respite. Prices go down as garden flowers, zinnias, Queen Anne's lace, stalky delphiniums, cornflowers, carnations, roses, roses, roses, and then some spring up.

Supply and demand dictate flower prices just as they do others. It is a fact of the florist's life that during the summer people buy fewer flowers. The reasons are obvious. Gardens and fields virtually burst with splendid and free offerings of flowers, weeds, and foliage. Then too the heat and languor of summer make indoor entertaining less inviting. Finally, summer flowers are easier to grow, which very much influences the price. With a reduced customer demand, growers and wholesalers gear their full flower inventories to the lucrative seasons, and florists are faced with a more limited choice. In turn, so are you, but what there is, is less costly. The exception is June, when you might want to avoid white flowers, unless you happen to be getting married. The traditional month for weddings keeps florists busy and the cost of white flowers climbing. (In December, the same applies to red flowers, so if you are in the mood to economize, think yellow.)

All Greens

Consider greens. Much more than an accessory, even though too often assigned that role, greens are an ample part of summer's bounty, and it is a time to give them their due. A splendid green arrangement has as much depth, variety of shapes, textures, and colors as one of flowers. Scale is easily achieved with greens, and the care of a large basket of foliage is minimal. Some types of foliage are more durable than others. Just remove the less lively foliage and replace it with new greens, or with leaves you can find at your florist's if you do not have a handy shrub to strip. Condition foliage in the same way you do flowers—unlike flowers, the entire green can be submerged in water—and use green foam if your container requires a holder. Among the most common foliage are: podocarpus, a bluish-green spiral stalk which lasts like iron; mag-

---

Opposite: Queen Anne's lace and blue and white delphiniums are part of summer's great bounty.

nolia; pittosporum, available in solid green and in variegated tones; boxwood; huckleberry; lemon leaves; and, of course, rhododendron, that ever-ready, ever-available, and low-priced filler. One of my favorites is eucalyptus, with its gray-green leaves that grow in a spiral or flat form. And how many leaves are there with a liniment scent? The flat eucalyptus, as it is known, has pliant seeded branches and enriches any array of greens or flowers. Once preserved or professionally dried, it is ideal for the spot where you do not want to use a fresh arrangement.

The versatility of green arrangements makes them serviceable in the best sense of the word. They can change from star to supporting player in an instant. A friend of mine keeps a large bowl of podocarpus in her living room and adds spider mums or lilies when the spirit moves her. In no time, and with little effort, she has a sizable array.

Fruits and Vegetables

Summer's trees bear fruit, and its vines, vegetables. Never mind that the florist's stock is depleted. Summer's outdoor larder overflows. There is a wealth of material about; indeed, anything that grows can be effectively used in a live arrangement — with or without flowers. Where the silk flower is inappropriate, the string of garlic is not. Needless to say, just as with people, some combinations are more compatible than others. The aubergine, or purple, of the eggplant takes to pinks and oranges, rosy leaves, and orange-yellow gourds, for instance. A bowl of various greens is the perfect foundation for such natural beauties as fluffy ruffled cabbage leaves, artichokes, a cluster of red radishes, chunky green peppers or slender hot ones, beet greens, pods, pieces of driftwood, and cattails. Seed heads add an extra bit of charm, while the openness of grasses imparts a lithe spirit. For a very rich quality, use the vibrant green of fresh parsley. By all means, be inventive. If your experiment pleases you, you have probably succeeded. If it does not, don't be disheartened. Try again. Playing with fantasy is always fun.

There is no gainsaying it, the little things in life become its luxuries. A day free of chores, an afternoon at the movies, breakfast in bed — ecstasy if prepared for you, blissful even if you must do it yourself. Set a morning tray with your prettiest crockery. Add color, and the touch that pampers, with a flower. For a container, I looked no further than the fruit basket. An apple is perfect, and it makes no difference if it is for baking, stewing, or eating raw. Core it deeply, insert a water-filled vial, and poke a flower — I chose a lily — through its rubber lid. Decorate the top with moss, if you wish. Should your appetite exceed the breakfast fare, there is always the apple.

Roses

Harebells and sweet lilies
show a thornless growth.
But the rose with all its
thorns excels them both.
— Christina Georgina
Rossetti

No other flower has been as extolled by poets or as studied by botanists. Indeed, the rose can claim the longest and most colorful history in the world of flowers.

This symbol of love, universal and most oft-used of flowers, is one of a large family of trees and shrubs called Rosaceae, which embraces the genera *Rubus* (raspberry, strawberry, blackberry, and other brambles), and *Prunus* (almond, apricot, nectarine, peach, and plum). The genus *Rosa* represents the rose, of which there are scores of known species.

From ancient days, the rose has been the stuff of illusion, fantasy, and literature. Pliny the Elder noted the belief in its curative powers, and listed 32 remedies brewed from its petals and leaves. Achilles' shield was decorated with roses. To Aphrodite roses were sacred, having sprung from the same foam of the sea which yielded her. Confucius tells us the library of the Emperor of China held some 600 volumes on the cultivation of roses. To the nobility of 5th-century China, use of the exquisite oil extracted from the roses in the Emperor's garden marked high birth, and was permitted only to the titled. Pity the poor commoner were he found with but a drop of the essence in his possession. His punishment was nothing less than death. And Nero found in the rose a weapon blessed from on high. Legend has it that he so thickly festooned the ceiling of his banquet hall with roses that the torrent of falling petals smothered his more unfortunate guests.

The rose reaches its zenith in early summer, and continues to bloom until the first frost. Roses should be cut in the late afternoon, and on the diagonal with a sharp knife. Do so when their buds are tight or, in the case of the large-headed, full varieties, when the flowers are only slightly open. Remove the leaves and thorns that will be below the waterline, and do use a preservative, as roses discharge more bacteria than most flowers.

The selection of roses is vast. Today's growers produce numerous hybrids in a multitude of colors. When buying roses, choose those still in bud if you want them to last, and check to make sure their necks (the tops of the stems) are sturdy, not limp.

Opposite: A small nosegay of sonia roses in my grandmother's lusterware sugar bowl accompanies a large bouquet of full-blown roses and Queen Anne's lace in an old mulberry ware coffeepot. A very Victorian setting.

Glorious as they are, rose heads are known to fall over long before their time has come. To restore such faded beauties, roll them in a tube of newspaper long enough to cover and support their heads. Recut the stems and dip them rapidly in boiling water, then let them rest for a bit in lukewarm water before arranging. The heat forces the flowers to draw water through their entire stems, and should strengthen their necks. It is not a foolproof method, but it usually works, and any effort to return a worthy queen to her throne is worth it.

Gladiolus

If there exists a misunderstood flower, it is the gladiolus. Its beauty is in its flower, not in its base, which, to be charitable, is uninteresting. Grown from corms (bulblike organs for the storage of food), gladioli appear in gardens from May to October and are available at florists year-round.

Because of the flower's swordlike leaves, Pliny the Elder coined the word *gladiolus*, from the Latin *gladius*, or sword. In their book *Flowers: A Guide For Your Garden*, Ippolito Pizzetti and Henry Cocker noted that, "In the language of flowers, the gladiolus represents pain and tears. . . . In ancient times, young men wore garlands of gladioli at the nuptials of a companion, as an expression of sorrow at losing the affection of a dear friend."

To condition gladioli, break off the tiny buds at the top of each stalk to allow the other flowers to open. When the lower flowers wilt, pull them off; the arrangement will live longer.

Gladioli are among the few flowers that do better in a small amount of water. Deep water weakens their stems and causes them to snap. However, I prefer my glads in a large round fishbowl in which the lower ones are angled in such a way that the bowl *must* be filled to the brim with water so all the stems are sure to get water. Most bulb or corm flowers do best in just two or three inches of water. If your glads do snap, they have probably had too much water. Never put glads in hot water, or the stems are sure to collapse. The same restriction applies to narcissi, tulips, and lilies.

A round Art Deco–style bowl is a splendid container for stalks of gladioli.

There are many gladiolus hybrids. The new miniature glads, although less hardy, are a lovely addition to a garden and come in as many interesting colors as the larger varieties. Maligned as they are, no other flower is as reasonably priced while being fairly hardy and lending itself to bouquets of a tremendous scale.

An interesting and economical use of glads that are a bit long in the tooth involves removing the dead matter, top and bottom. If one fresh blossom remains, and it happens to be in the middle of the stalk, simply cut the upper stem just above the healthy flower — the cut will not show — then cut the stem again a few inches below the flower. You will now have a single regal gladiolus. Put it in a small glass bottle and you might find people asking the name of such an unusually pretty flower.

Symbolically the gladiolus also stands for generosity, so be generous, in turn, and do not snub it. True, it has flaws, but as we all know, a few clever tricks can disguise even the homeliest feature.

4
Autumn

Bronze, orange, vivid yellow, pale pink, deep rose, lilac pink, magenta, wine red, and green-white. It must be autumn. At no other time of year are we dazzled by such a sweep of color. It is nature at her most brazen.

Chrysanthemums reign, as they have for centuries. Originally Chinese, this flower is so esteemed by the Japanese, and primary in their gardens, that they crowned it *Kiku*, or "Queen of the East." Many splendid varieties offer a wide choice of shapes, sizes, and colors. At the head of the chrysanthemum family is the outsized "football" mum, one large flower on a single stalk. Included in the family's many types are spider mums and rover mums, statesmen, daisy pompons, and cushion pompons—but pompons are a bit different, as they have branchlike stalks that bear many florets. Thus there is the spider mum and the spider pompon. The robustness of mums makes them among the most frequently grown of flowering plants.

Before arranging mums, break, scrape, and split the fibrous stems (or hammer them), and remove most of the foliage, as it dries up well before the flower wilts. Cut mums will last up to three weeks.

Autumn does not deprive us of lilies. Florists stock numerous varieties all year, but many are still available in the garden. Orange lilies are plentiful, and tend to be less expensive than their kin.

A unique way to handle lilies involves a bit of deception. Take a clay pot, line it with two plastic bags (the second one is for extra security), put a brick of wet green foam in the liner, and top it with a layer of well-dampened moss. Now you are ready to poke your tall, conditioned lilies into the moss-covered surface. One to three stalks makes the arrangement look natural. (Lily bulbs usually produce only a few flower spikes.) *Voilà*—a creation that looks for all the world like a pot of growing lily plants. My fake lily plants often seem fresher than real lily plants, because I can use lily blooms at just the right stage of development. (Remember to keep the green foam wet.)

Opposite: This array of chrysanthemums, photographed in the flower market, shows a few of the many varieties of mums and pompons available today.

47

Dried
Flowers

Some people like them, and some do not. No matter. It is never a question of good taste or bad. Dried flowers not only have a character distinctly their own, but the art of drying them is an increasingly popular hobby. Satisfying though it is, it takes time, space, and patience. Annuals grown in sunny places lend themselves best to drying—roses, for instance, statice, cornflowers (often called bachelor's buttons), zinnias, and my favorite, hydrangea.

There are three ways to dry flowers: air drying, sand drying, and silica gel drying. (Silica gel is absorbent, and resembles coarse white sand.) Borax, a white crystalline salt, can be substituted for either sand or silica gel. Although it can be used alone, it works rapidly, and hence is difficult to control. A more practical solution is to mix one part of sand to two parts of borax. Whichever method you use, choose perfect flowers; bruises are exaggerated in the drying. Their petals should have no excessive moisture, and the flowers' development should not be far advanced, as it continues while drying.

The easiest procedure is air drying, which can take days to weeks, depending on the flower. It also produces the finest results, probably because it is the most natural means. Particularly good for air drying are: larkspur, statice, delphinium, goldenrod, allium, fatheaded yarrow, and pussy willow. Secure small bunches of branches or flowers with rubber bands; wire is not advisable as the stems contract while drying and the flowers can come loose. Find a dry, dark, warm spot in which to dry them and, to ensure straight stems, hang the bunches upside down on a hook by the rubber band. Flowers dried by air last well, and are less likely to absorb normal air moisture (humidity) which can make them sag or collapse.

For flowers that cannot be air dried, such as peonies, roses, and tulips, try sand or silica gel. Sand is the heaviest and slowest desiccant (drying agent)—it takes about three weeks, and mutes the flower's original color—but it is inexpensive and gives good support to flowers, which can be left in it indefinitely. If the sand is sifted between procedures it can be used forever, as can silica gel.

Opposite: Pots of cut orange mid-century lilies in green foam make this bedroom sitting area even cozier.

One note of caution: The weight of sand makes it inappropriate for very fragile flowers, and with *all* flowers it must be used with a delicate hand.

While sand is non-absorbent, silica gel and borax hasten the drying process by absorbing water from the flowers. (With borax, roses can dry in 12 hours, cornflowers in 36 hours. Large blossoms take a few weeks.) A helpful guideline for silica gel is: Two days for thin-petaled flowers such as daisies, four to five days for the fleshier tulip or peony, a week or more for a flower as dense as a rose. In all cases, flowers should be completely buried in very dry sand, or silica gel. To preserve the flower's shape, pour the materials with care. Keep a vigilant eye on those immersed in silica gel or borax, and do not overdry the flowers or they will appear scorched and shrunken. The cobalt usually added to silica gel acts as a handy signal. Its bright blue fades when the mixture has absorbed its capacity of moisture. Remove the flowers at this point.

After drying, the flowers will have a light coating of sand, silica gel, or borax. The sand can be knocked off easily, but the silica gel or borax might have to be removed with a small paintbrush. It can be tedious, but it is important. If the powders are not removed they continue to absorb the little moisture left in the flower and overdry it. Silica gel, unlike sand, yields vivid colors, sometimes even more radiant than the original. (Store silica gel and borax in airtight containers so they do not absorb the air's moisture.)

If you decide to wire flowers before drying to prevent their heads from snapping off, remember not to extend the wire too high through the top of the flower, as the heads shrink while drying and the wire might be exposed. (See the section on Nosegays for directions on wiring.)

When all is said and done, the simplest flower to dry is baby's breath: Cut the stems. Stand them in water. Let the water evaporate. DRIED BABY'S BREATH.

Charming as they are, dried flowers do attract dust and can take on a tired and dreary cast. Blow on them if you wish, but sadly they cannot really be cleaned. Either change them, or perk up

---

Opposite: These crates of dried flowers are only some of the vast inventory of dried material on the market today.

the arrangement by adding new dried material, silk foliage, or silk flowers. The description of flowers as silk, by the way, is deceptive. Flowers today are made from a wide variety of cloths and synthetic fabrics and, hence, are more reasonable than silk ones, which are almost as dear as they are beautiful. They are easily arranged in Styrofoam—also used to hold dried material—which can be hidden with moss.

Although cloth flowers are not a substitute for living ones, a clever friend of mine keeps a few pretty ones on hand and in an emergency mixes them judiciously with fresh flowers. Her results are startingly attractive. The trick is to flesh out the real thing with only a few counterfeits.

Preserved Greens

Foliage can be preserved nicely by slitting the stems of greens and standing them in a mixture of one part glycerin to three parts lukewarm water. The process takes about a month, and is completed when the tops of the greens have changed color somewhat. This indicates that the glycerin mixture has been drawn through the stem and has replaced the water in the greens. Remove them from the solution, wipe them off, and you will have flexible, sturdy, preserved greens. Magnolia, autumn leaves, galax leaves, and many other types of foliage are easily preserved with the glycerin treatment. The greens, however, are apt to take on a brownish cast.

The birch branches in this 19th-century Chinese vase need no light or water. A very welcome practical arrangement.

5
Winter

Nature lives even in the dead of winter. It arrives officially December 21st, and thanks to rapid global transportation, so do a host of familiar and unusual flowers from warmer climes. Carnations by the armful, white pompons, chincherinchee (also called Star of Bethlehem), branches of quince, greens, plants, plants, plants, and then some.

As vast parts of the world lie white and shorn outside, indoors is alive with the warmth of cut flowers, forced bulbs, and early flowering branches.

'Tis also the season to be jolly, thoughtful, and festive. The eight days of Hanukkah, the twelve days of Christmas, the hours of New Year's, teem with celebration, scents, and symbols.

One of the most familiar is the Christmas tree. If you have a living one, before setting it up and decorating it, test it by pulling the branches. If the needles fall, the tree is past its prime. Recut, or, more accurately, resaw the trunk to expose new cells through which the tree can draw water.

One Christmas I decorated a pine tree with tiny white lights, then filled small flower vials — which I ornamented with ribbons and netting — with chincherinchee flowers, and wired them to the tree's branches with green floral tape. I also added vials of baby's breath. The effect was glorious, and lo and behold, the flowers stayed fresh until it was time to take the tree down.

Another beautiful tree on which several of us collaborated was covered with little white lights, and fruit we wired to the tree. We used all manner of fruit — nothing esoteric, just what the greengrocer happened to have in stock. Some fruits we clustered together, others we used by themselves, and all of them stood up for more than a week.

Winter, by the way, is an ideal time to mix fresh fruit and leaves in a basket to use as a centerpiece. For extra height, put a kitchen bowl upside down in the basket, mound plump green grapes on top, and stick branches of leaves between the clusters of grapes.

Opposite: A glorious collection of flowering plants brings a holiday spirit to this foyer. Poinsettia, amaryllis, and azalea plants, and a single narcissus bulb, are all in moss-covered pots tied with strands of raffia. The baskets are woven wisteria vines.

Another traditional symbol of the season is the poinsettia. Poinsettia plants are good alone or en masse. A basket of several small ones in four-inch pots, surrounded by short branches of pine, is a colorful centerpiece.

To set a festive holiday table, put a single pointsettia flower in a clear glass vase in front of each guest. When you cut poinsettia flowers, you must stop the stem from bleeding its milky sap. Singe the end of the stem with a flame, push the stem into sand, or plug the end with a clot of dry green foam.

The poinsettia is a hardy and long-lasting houseplant when properly treated—which means no fumes, drafts, direct sunlight, or excessive heat. As the plant's roots must be moist at all times, a plastic (non-absorbent) pot is usually the best container. When your poinsettia gets "leggy" in the summer, cut the leaves back, repot it, and from September through October consistently alternate ten hours or so of bright indirect sunlight with fourteen hours of absolute darkness. If you follow this routine, your poinsettia should rebloom for the next holiday season.

Now that we are so conscious of nutrition, plants have superseded chocolates as the gift for all seasons, particularly the winter holiday season. The kalanchoe, cyclamen, gloxinia, and azalea are especially favored. The kalanchoe has clusters of tiny deep-orange, greenish-white, pink, or yellow flowers, which last several weeks but are long outlived by their green foliage. The gloxinia, with its large leaves and velvety flowers in rich and vivid colors, is pure luxury. Keep the soil barely moist by adding water to the saucer under the pot. Do not overwater, and never allow the plant to sit in water for long periods. Once the blossoms fade, gloxinias need a dormant period; gradually decrease the waterings to nothing and let the plants rest dry for a few months, when new blossoms will appear.

The cyclamen plant, with its heart-shaped leaves, requires good ventilation, plenty of moisture—created by watering from underneath—and a *cool* room, approximately 65° (Fahrenheit).

Very simply, azaleas are great houseplants, and with the development of so many hybrids an endless variety is available. Those

An upside-down garden box is the base for this Christmas tree decorated with fruits, ribbons, and small white lights. Pots of narcissus bulbs complete the setting.

grown in greenhouses are usually pink, deep pink (florists insist on saying red), red-orange, and white. The yellow and pure orange varieties are grown indoors. If the plant is not soaked the roots and blossoms will shrivel, so do douse it generously, then keep it moist and in a cool, very light spot, particularly in the bud stage. It is normal for the old leaves to drop, but not the new ones. If new leaves are falling, the azalea is getting too much water, or too little light. To prevent red spider mites, occasionally dunk the foliage in warm sudsy water; however, should your efforts be for nought and mites appear, use a miticide — available at most florists.

To sum up some general rules: All flowering houseplants should be kept moist-to-wet, from the bud stage to the flower stage; all need to be fertilized; all should be set in indirect light, away from drafts and fumes. Once plants are through blooming, they should be repotted in a container one inch larger than the original. Much like any move, repotting is a trauma for plants — and sometimes for you — and they require a quiet period followed by a dormant one. During this time they use less water, but special care should be taken to give them their prescribed doses of sunlight and total darkness.

It may not be your notion of fun, but forcing bulbs *is* fun. Then, too, bulb plants make lovely gifts.

Lilies of the valley are quickly forced. Buy pips (single rootstocks), at your nursery. Plant them loosely in a mixture of one part peat moss, one part sand, and place the pots in a cool, dark spot for three to five weeks. During the rooting period keep the plants moist, and never allow them to dry out. After three weeks or more, poke the soil with your finger to feel for root development. Once the roots have appeared, your plants are ready to be placed in a sunny spot. Again, keep them moist. In a matter of days, you should see flowers.

Tulips, narcissus, hyacinth, crocus, and amaryllis are also easily forced, although the rooting period is 15 weeks. Here's how:

Cover the bottom of a container with potting soil. Do not bury the entire bulb in the soil; some of it should be visible. Begin the forcing process by simulating winter, storing the bulbs for 15 weeks in a cool place — 45° to 60°; the refrigerator is good if you

Lit candles and pots of glorious white amaryllis in full bloom create a warm spirit for a holiday evening.

have the room and, most important, if you will remember to keep the bulbs moist. (The amaryllis bulb is an exception, and should not be refrigerated. Just keep it on a counter.) At the end of this stage the bulbs are ready for a bit of sunshine; a cool windowsill is fine. Once a bud appears, the bulb needs bright, indirect light, and should be kept moist as well as cool.

Although it is possible to induce a bulb to rebloom indoors, bulbs can be recalcitrant, so do not be disheartened if your best efforts fail. When the blossom is gone, cut back the flower stalk, but leave the foliage; once the leaves turn yellow, water the bulb less. When the soil is completely dry, store the bulb in a cool, dry spot. With luck, the cycle begins again.

The amaryllis, which grows from a large bulb (the larger the bulb, the larger the flowers it produces), usually has two stalks, each with two to four blooms. The first appears several days before the second. Using a pot slightly larger than the bulb, to which you have added pot shards or a few pebbles at the bottom for extra drainage, carefully embed the bulb's roots in the soil. Amaryllis bulbs like tight quarters, and should be planted in individual pots. Leave some of the bulb visible. Pack the dirt firmly but gently, so the fragile roots are not damaged. Water until there is seepage from the bottom of the pot; with the first growth, water again.

Amaryllis bulbs are unpredictable. Some sprout quickly, others come along only when they see fit. Most often the flower bud appears before the leaves, which develop as the first bud is opening. When the amaryllis does bud, it needs plenty of water, plant food monthly, and a few hours of sunshine daily.

Holiday Time

Deck the halls with boughs of holly, garlands of princess pine roping, mistletoe, and pine boughs. It would scarcely be Christmas without them. To keep them looking fresh throughout the season, there are a few tricks you can use. Princess pine roping, made with branches of a fluffy, supple evergreen, should be slightly damp and dark green when it is bought. Soak it overnight in the bathtub in room-temperature water. If you are so inclined, you can make your own roping by winding heavy cord, or flexible wire of medium gauge, around evergreen branches; long-needled pine is fine for roping. Keep all evergreens as cool and damp as possible, misting them often.

A basket of holly makes a simple and tasteful Christmas arrangement. As holly branches, both green and variegated, dry quickly once indoors, spray a clear varnish on both sides of the leaves to seal in the moisture. Putting holly in water is useless, as it does not draw well, and the leaves can drop more quickly.

Opposite: A wreath of birch twigs hangs over this gala Christmas mantle with its handmade stockings, moss-covered baskets with birch twig handles, rubrum lily heads, heather, euphorbia branches, princess pine roping, red orchid branches, and English variegated holly.

Do not blame your florist if your holly has no berries; holly plants are male and female, and only the female yields berries. Holly (or ilex) is actually an evergreen shrub or tree, with some reaching heights of 20 feet. Superstition has it that holly brings luck if taken into the house Christmas Eve — not before — and kept until Twelfth Night, when it is burned. Try it. Maybe it is so.

Holiday decorations, especially those you make, are charming and thoughtful gifts. Two particularly welcome ones are a mistletoe ball and a twig wreath. They take time, but it is time pleasantly spent.

For centuries mistletoe has been many things to many people. To me it is a plant with pale yellow-green leaves and waxy berries — not very pretty, until its parts are fashioned into a ball. Technically it is an aerial parasite, attaching itself to treetops by its roots — it is partial to apple trees. It seems the custom of kissing under mistletoe branches began with the Druids, who held the plant sacred. Today the reverence is gone, but the tradition lingers. Hence, the ever-popular mistletoe ball.

Mistletoe Ball

Take half a standard brick of well-soaked heavy-duty green foam and twist chicken wire around it to enclose it in a cage, or box. On one side, attach a 10-inch length of medium-gauge wire with which to hold the cage while making the ball, and later to hang the finished ball. (You can easily conceal the wire by wrapping it with ribbon.)

Cut a large bunch of boxwood into sprigs of two to four inches in length, and poke the sprigs through the spaces in the wire into the foam. Turn the ball as you do this, so no spots are missed. Spray varnish the boxwood ball at this point.

Twist pieces of wire around small shoots of mistletoe, and allow enough extra wire to insert them in the foam between the clusters of boxwood. Leave the ball as is, or decorate it with ribbons and holly. Now all that remains is to choose the spot in your home where you want to be kissed.

Succulent Wreath

An inventive lady in California constructs a long-lasting succulent wreath, popular in warmer climes, in which the plants are actually rooted. Place a wire frame on top of several large layers of well-soaked moss and fill the entire frame with rich potting soil (approximately four cups of soil for a sizable 16-inch frame). Bring the moss up and over the frame and bind with floral wire or floral tape, in effect creating a sausage of moss. With an ice pick, or any sharp pointed tool, make holes in the moss frame and insert about two inches of the stem of each succulent. (Pick your succulents a week before you plan to use them, so their stems have a chance to rest and harden.) Secure the succulents to the moss frame with ordinary hairpins. Voilà, a most out-of-the-ordinary wreath.

Wreaths can be made from just about anything to suit just about any taste: evergreens fixed to a heavy wire ring; a kitchen wreath, ready to be stripped when needed, of bay leaves, rosemary, and thyme attached to a moss-covered wire ring; fruits made fast to a Styrofoam ring, tied in turn to a wire ring. (It is possible to use a Styrofoam ring alone, but the wire adds support for the fruit's weight.) They can be sophisticated or homespun, lush or stark, green, blue, purple, or all three together.

Wreath of Twigs

A few suggested materials are birch branches, cherry branches, grapevines, and bittersweet vines.

Select one flexible branch of medium thickness. (If the branch or twig is not flexible, soak it for several hours in hot water.) Make a round shape, being certain the ends of the branch overlap one another. Wire the ends together, or tie them with string. Now you have the basic frame. (Number 1 in the illustration.)

Weave twigs into the frame, adjusting the twigs to make your wreath more circular as you go. (Number 2 in the illustration.) Stems of weeds and heavy grasses can be added for a rustic touch. Don't fret if the wreath is not a perfect circle. Its beauty is in its irregularity and natural character.

Make a circle and tie the ends if necessary. Inserting the thick end of each twig into the frame first, weave additional twigs until the wreath has the desired thickness.

63

Carnations

Despite the dream of Karl Marx, there is simply no such society as a classless one, even among flowers. Pity the poor carnation, long dismissed by the elite as ordinary. I heartily disagree. So did the English statesman and writer William Corbett, who, in 1821, exclaimed: "I hesitate not a moment to prefer the plant of a fine carnation, to a gold watch set with diamonds."

Neither was it belittled by the Greeks, who named it *Dianthus* (pink) *Caryophyllus*, because its scent resembled the spice caryophyllus, commonly called clove. Through time it came to be known as carnation, and acquired a distinguished history.

In the 1200s, the Muslims of North Africa spiced their drinks with carnation, while French Crusaders found relief from the heat and stench of Tunis by adding the flowers to cooling tonics. The soldiers of the French prince and general, "the Great Condé," wore carnations as a symbol of valor, and Napoleon chose carnation red as the color for the Legion of Honor ribbon. Today the carnation, "winter's flower," symbolizes the month of January, as well it might — for its blooming period spans October to the end of March. And its fragrance is still widely used in perfume.

There are some 2,000 varieties of carnations, often called pinks, and all are distinguished by notched stems that are swollen at the nodes. Sweet william and baby's breath are members of the carnation's extended family.

Carnations are most accommodating. They mix comfortably with other flowers, and stand equally well on their own. Cut their stems above the stem joints, and condition them in a bucket of lukewarm water up to their heads. Very tight and undeveloped carnations can be put in hot water. When you use the branchy miniature carnations, cut off the small side shoots to give the main stalk added strength.

Florist's carnations are grown in South America, California, and Florida, then boxed and shipped while the buds are still tight and latent. (When they are ready to be marketed, the wholesaler cuts the stems, and forces the flowers open by plunging them in hot water.) If your carnations are tighter than you would like when you buy them, blow on the flower head — warm breath causes the

On any day of the year, a wealth of miniature carnations in myriad colors can be found in the flower market, where florists make their selections.

petals to open — and gently spread the outer petals with your fingers.

Carnations are one of the few flowers that can be easily dyed — an abomination to a purist — and what would St. Patrick's Day be without a green carnation? The dye, added to hot water, is drawn through the flower's capillaries and transforms a white carnation into a green one. The stem remains *au naturel.*

Do not be outwitted by a ruse of the trade. Some wily florists are known to dye old flowers, or spray them with a tint, to make them more salable. The knowledgeable consumer checks the base of the stem for clues — a flower dyed green, for example, will have a green cast to its base.

6

Special Occasions

When words fail, there are flowers. Their delicate perfection makes them a time-honored way to say: "I care."

Special occasions are celebrated with special drinks, special food, and special people in a special place. Valentine's Day is one such occasion. Take champagne, add dinner for two in an intimate setting, festoon it with a colossal red balloon tied to a basket of flowers, and create a visual fantasia.

Thanksgiving Day is yet another special time, and the centerpiece for the table is almost as traditional as the food—a bowl of bronze, yellow, rust, and magenta mums surrounded by variegated leaves. A simple design of blue and yellow flowers, or red and orange ones, is fitting for a bar mitzvah. The ruby wedding anniversary, hailed in the fortieth year, calls for the obvious ruby-red flowers, while ten years later, the silver anniversary fete can be decorated with silver bowls of white flowers. By custom, Easter flowers are white, and the Easter lily itself the one most often used; the white auratum lily is beautiful but expensive.

When the night abounds with tricksters, proffer a treat—a Halloween dinner. Hollow out a pumpkin, line it with a container that holds water, add your flowers, and you have a jovial centerpiece for the table. (Put the pumpkin on a clear glass plate to protect the table from the pumpkin's moisture.)

There are no decisions to be made about the Fourth of July—red sweetheart roses, blue cornflowers, and white daisies spilling out from a picnic basket add spirit to an evening of fireworks.

Many years spent creating parties for myself and others have taught me many lessons. At a large gathering, such as a cocktail party, group numbers of light-colored flowers—inexpensive ones are fine—in places where they are easily seen by standing guests. For the smaller party—a seated dinner, for instance—where guests are closer to the flowers, fewer and more interesting arrangements are appropriate.

And do not neglect the entryway. In effect, its looks are your words of greeting. Guests feel particularly welcome when it, too, is special.

Opposite: This apartment's library is a fine setting for a very special Valentine's Day surprise supper for two, complete with champagne and a helium-filled balloon.

Weddings

Phalaenopsis *orchids, stephanotis, roses, freesia, and ivy — carefully wired individually and then wired together — compose this traditional bridal bouquet.*

They may not be the stars of the ceremony, but they are distinguished supporting players. Weddings and flowers are almost synonymous. As there are many ways to successfully decorate a room, so too there are many ways to orchestrate a beautiful wedding, be it simple or grand. Each wedding is unique, but here are some suggestions as a *general* guide.

Church or Temple Flowers

Altar Flowers: Assuming the church or temple permits altar flowers, and most do with the exception of the Catholic Church, two vases of white or light-colored flowers are always lovely, as is a large bowl in the center of the altar, if the Bible is kept elsewhere. The flowers need not be terribly fancy, but arrangements should be expansive.

In the Catholic Church, an oversized glass bowl on the floor in front of the altar can look well if the church is fairly small; however, a pair of ample arrangements on wire stanchions, or on tables in front and slightly to the side of the altar, are far more visible.

Pew Ribbons: I particularly like white bows tied on the side of every third or fourth pew, in addition to the customary ribbons on the front and back pews. Often I ornament the ribbons with flowers, such as lily of the valley, poking from the tops of the bows. I firmly believe the church should look different than it does on Sunday mornings, so guests immediately know it is to a wedding they are going.

Candles: After five o'clock in the winter and six in the summer, candles are appropriate. Many temples and churches own candle stanchions that can be borrowed. They can be adorned with strings of greens to which flowers can always be added.

Flowers for the Bride and Groom and the Bridal Party

The Bride: Be it a first, second, or third marriage, the bride's flowers are most often white. In the bouquet shown, each flower is wired and can actually be moved to give either an open or a tight look. The traditional flower is stephanotis, small and sweet smelling, but the more mature bride of 28-years-plus might prefer a branch of orchids tied with a ribbon.

The Groom and His Groomsmen, including Fathers: A simple boutonniere of stephanotis, a single white rosebud, or a white carnation is fitting.

Bridesmaids: Baskets of loose flowers or a few lilies tied with ribbons might be fancied by younger bridesmaids, while attendants of the bride with white orchids could carry colored orchid branches. Nosegays, or wired bouquets, are suitable for bridesmaids of all ages. Flower colors should match those of the dresses; white flowers are never appropriate for bridesmaids.

Hair flowers, for the bride and bridesmaids, can be a single cymbidium, a piece of freesia, or a stem of baby's breath tied to hair combs. For flower girls, charming headbands can be fashioned with dainty dendrobia orchids, and strands of baby ivy leaves.

Reception and Cake Flowers

Create an inviting ambiance at the entrance to the reception area with a pretty bouquet of flowers. Location and budget can dictate the choice of flowers for inside, which need not be coordinated with the color of the bridesmaids' dresses.

Most bakers will embed a small vase or drinking glass in the top layer of the wedding cake to hold a few miniature roses, or small flowers that pick up the color of the frosting decoration. The base of the cake can also be surrounded with greens and flowers, but they should never overwhelm the cake.

Nosegays and Corsages

A. To make a nosegay or corsage, wire and cover each flower stem with floral tape. The stems of the flowers are then taped together.

B. A finished carnation corsage.

A nosegay is a small bouquet of flowers, and usually carried in the hands; a corsage is a small bouquet to be worn. Both must be made by wiring individual flowers, which are then taped together to form the bouquet. Any flower in need of wiring, whether a delicate one for a nosegay, or a larger one for a full arrangement, is wired in the same way.

Cut a four- to five-inch piece of green-covered medium-gauge straight wire. Carefully stick the end of it directly under the head of the flower and push it up through the head, holding the remaining wire parallel to the stem. Now grasp the neck of the flower and gingerly twist the rest of the wire around the stem. Wiring is excellent for those flowers whose heads flop over because they are too heavy for their stems—asters, gerbera, parrot tulips, and some varieties of roses, for example. It is also an effective way to resurrect a broken flower. A hollow-stemmed zinnia can be so bent it will not draw water; once it is wired it has a normal life span.

If you are making a nosegay or corsage, after wiring the flowers cover the entire wired area with green, nonsticky floral tape. (It stays in place once it is pulled and twisted around the stem.) If you want to use more than one flower in a corsage, wire and tape each flower individually, and tape the stems together with floral tape. Always handle flower heads gently to avoid bruising them.

A proper corsage pin, by the way, has an oblong-shaped head, while a boutonniere pinhead is round.

A useful trick when constructing a nosegay or corsage is to substitute wet pipe cleaners for wire. The fuzzy coating, which is hidden by the floral tape, retains water and keeps flowers fresh longer. I always use pipe cleaners with stephanotis, as their small stems (which provide nourishment) usually break off.

Anemones and Topiary Tree

Anemones and heather bedeck the top of this mossed topiary, while its bamboo trunk is ringed with heather and streamers of raffia.

For a flower of so fragile a cast, it is heavy with history. In the Bible it is the "lily of the field"; in Christian imagery it symbolizes the crucifixion; early Byzantine mosaics picture Christ amid fields of them. It is the anemone, or wind flower, as it is also known. Its name sprang from the Greek *anemos*, or wind, recording the fact that these colorful flowers are opened by the wind. A member of the buttercup family, it is a perennial herb. Legends tell us the Romans used it to prevent fevers, while others believed freckles would disappear with an application of anemones. The brilliant red variety is said to have been born of the blood of Adonis, dying in a meadow of white anemones.

There are ninety species of the genus *Anemone*, but the most familiar is the anemone coronaria, or poppy anemone, a favorite garden plant. This black-centered flower grows in shades of lavender, purple, scarlet, pink, white, and rosy mauve. Cut its stems with a knife, give them plenty of water, and place them in a *cool* room. If possible, avoid using green foam to hold anemones; they do not draw water particularly well from it and they are big drinkers. The day after arranging your anemones, add more water to the container.

Anemones are available from florists from October through April, and are costly when first on the market. By the end of their season they are relatively inexpensive; however, like all flowers at the end of their tether, they are less hardy. The cut December anemone will last five days in water; the April anemone survives only two days.

Topiary. The dictionary defines it as "the art of trimming and training shrubs or trees into unnatural ornamental shapes." For this book I define it as a tree made of greens and/or flowers. It is simple to do and produces a choice bouquet.

Fill a container (a flowerpot is particularly good) with cement, or plaster of paris mixed with water. Before it has set completely, press a dowel stick or clean branch into the mixture. This becomes the tree trunk. For the treetop, push a ball of Styrofoam, or one of heavy-duty green foam covered with chicken wire, onto the tree trunk. The green foam can be soaked or dry. If it is dry, put the flowers in water-filled aqua picks before poking them in the foam. (I usually cover the foam with moss.) As wet green foam tends to drip, dry foam is preferable even though using it with aqua picks makes it more time consuming.

If the top is a Styrofoam ball, wire the flowers onto sticks first and then poke them directly into the ball. Be certain the flowers are robust, such as pompons. For the smaller topiary tree, a potato serves as an excellent base for greens and flowers, and its tendency to retain water is an added advantage. Paint the dowel tree trunk, or sheathe it in ribbons; leave the trunk fashioned from a branch just as it is.

Surprise Element

What nicer surprise than to be given what we heroically refrain from giving ourselves. Flowers, for instance. And almost as gratifying is doing the same for others. The gift could be a basket of cattails gathered in the country, or a bunch of lilies of the valley tied to a friend's doorknob to say welcome home. Gifts of flowers flatter and pamper — and who among us is so grown up that we do not respond?

There are as many reasons for the surprise gift of flowers as there are flower varieties — a birthday, an anniversary, I'm glad, I'm sorry, a goodbye, a hello. Or perhaps the best of all reasons — because I like doing it.

Often I send flowers to friends after going to their home for dinner, and sometimes even before going. A bouquet of flowers and a thank-you note to your host or hostess are always correct. Actually, even more than correct; they are thoughtful, and a special surprise.

A basket of white and yellow flowers in an early spring bouquet welcomes guests in Laguna Beach, California.

7
Creating Moods

At the very least, flowers have been footnotes throughout recorded history. For centuries, in many civilizations and in many cultures, they have enriched the quality of life. The early Chinese adorned their temple altars with vases of cut flowers; the ancient Egyptians arrayed them on banquet tables, carried them in processions, and offered them to their dead. Romans fashioned wreaths and chaplets of flowers and greens, and wrapped their pillars with garlands. So too did the Greeks. Tall, formally arranged cones of flowers, fruits, and greens were much admired by the Byzantines.

About A.D. 1000 churches and monasteries began to play a major role in the cultivation of flowers. Their gardens burst with flowers and countless herbs to be used in medicines, with food, and as adornment.

In the 14th century, medieval dourness gave way to the Italian Renaissance, and with it came a rebirth of the art of flower arranging, which achieved new heights not only in Italy but in much of Europe. Botticelli, Titian, and Tintoretto were only a few of the Italian masters to paint the richly colored and popular flowers. The art of 17th- and 18th-century France shows a fondness for tight, oval-shaped, and highly stylized arrangements, with each flower so fastidiously placed it could be seen individually. The more casual bouquets of loosely arranged and gaily colored flowers, on the other hand, mark the style of the Dutch and Flemish schools of the 17th and early 18th centuries.

If there will always be an England, there will always be an English garden. Their collective green thumb is legendary. In fact and fiction, the English country house abounds with glorious bouquets, and always has. As flower arrangements tend to reflect the tone of the period, and formality was a keynote of the Georgian years (1714 to 1830), designs were restrained and ceremonious, only to become more casual in the ensuing Regency period. The Victorians loved opulence—furniture ornately carved, fabrics in rich patterns, lush dark-colored blossoms arrayed lavishly. Men wore flowers in their

---

Opposite: This large arrangement of French silk flowers and dried material was designed by Jeanne Cameron Shanks for the Grand Salon of the American Embassy residence in Paris. The flowers' colors are drawn from those in the Chinese screen.

buttonholes, while women fastened them in their hair and to their bosoms. Victorian ladies often carried a "posy" in a holder fashioned from precious metal or porcelain, the precursor of today's nosegay.

Flower arranging is not a haphazard art. It has a heritage, in the Far East and in Europe, from which Americans have drawn attitudes and styles and adapted them to a new and different world.

Japanese Flower Arranging

To enter the world of *ikebana*, the art of Japanese flower arranging, is a unique experience for the Westerner. *Ikebana* — "the arrangement of living material" — began many centuries ago in the Buddhist temples, with its basic rules laid down by a priest, Ono-no-Imoko. In essence, the arrangement symbolized the living universe, spiritually and physically, and the construction of it was to be approached with a peaceful mind, as it was considered a form of prayer or meditation. The quality of tranquility is still fundamental.

There are four basic types of *ikebana* styles. (The *kenzan*, or pinholder, is the arranger most commonly used for any of them.)

I. *Rikka* or *rikkwa*: Translated as "standing flowers," this refers to the early temple arrangements, often as tall as six feet, which were constructed by priests.

II. *Shoka*: This classical style evolved at the end of the 17th century. As in all *ikebana* styles, *shoka* represents the three main aspects of the universe — *ten-chi-sin*, or heaven, earth, man. The tallest stem is the *shin* (heaven), always positioned first. Its height must measure twice the combined total of the height and diameter of the vase. The mid-length branch, the *soe* (man), is placed second, and is three quarters the length of the *shin*. The third and shortest stem is the *hikka* (earth), which is three quarters the length of the *soe*. Only when this is in place are supplementary stems, called *jushi*, added to the arrangement. These proportions apply to both curved and straight stems, and to all *ikebana* styles.

A shoka *arrangement of iris in a Japanese vase. It is customary to set a round container on a square or rectangular base. If possible, Japanese arrangements should be placed against a plain wall.*

III. *Nagiere*: Translated as "thrown in," this form is a simplification of the *shoka*. Shaped in upright containers, it is more adaptable to home settings than the treelike *rikka*.

IV. *Moribana*: This is the most used of all the *ikebana* styles. Introduced in 1910, *moribana*, or "built up flowers," requires a flat container ample enough to create a scene within it—mountains, valleys, a lake, perhaps an island. *Moribana* can assume an upright or a slanted form.

Symbolism is all-important in *ikebana*, and there are specific, not rigid, meanings. In general, grass and branches are masculine, flowers are feminine. Lines that droop are sad; those that curve are happy. A bare branch denotes winter, a black stem with blossoms signals spring, and a thickly foliated stem symbolizes summer.

In sum, the study of *ikebana* is a way to understand the natural world, and the practice of it is a spiritual exercise.

Lady's Desk; Man's Library

A house "decorated" with flowers is more a showcase than a home. The most natural use of flowers and plants is always the best; here a bud vase with a rose, there a flowering plant in a basket, elsewhere, if not everywhere, a bowl of gladioli. The style of an arrangement is defined by the setting in which it is placed, and a harmony of parts is the goal.

To design an arrangement with a modern feeling, for instance, use a simple, straight-lined container and simple flowers. A mass of large flowers, all alike, in a stark glass vase, gives such an impression. So does a small black vase, shaped like a ball, holding one short-stemmed and full-blown white peony. Its directness is a touch of perfection in a pure white modern room.

A. The flowers on the lady's 18th-century English desk, on the right, should be in keeping with the mementos displayed there. An arrangement's scale, the choice of container, the color of the flowers used, are determined by the objects already in place. While solutions are not always obvious, mistakes often can be. A large and dramatic arrangement would overpower the cherished photograph of little girls and the delicate Chinese lamp. Hence, for the desk shown, the all-white nosegay and its vase were carefully selected to integrate with the collection, and to reflect its spirit.

B. If flowers can be of one or the other gender, so too can those who enjoy them. A man's library is just as fitting a stage for flowers as a lady's boudoir. They are not a woman's prerogative.

The furnishings of a room tell you how to adorn it. Modern rooms and tailored ones call for plants, and sculptural arrangements of flowers. A large cactus plant is a handsome addition to a sparsely furnished modern living room, but would be sadly miscast in a Victorian drawing room of patterns and bric-a-brac.

Although the pumpkin-colored library is not modern, its air is masculine, and the cluster of sweet william arranged in a sculptural round shape on the coffee table seems correct. To the eye, the weight of the clump of flowers matches that of the boxes, while the blossoms' colors blend with the deep wine hues in the leather sofas. The parts unite to create a strong image.

A. I love flowers in all bedrooms, mine, my children's, the guest room. But not very formal or very large arrangements, which never look right. Instead, I put a single flower in a small glass beaker, or, as in this guest room, a large airy bouquet of tiny wild daisies and Railroad Annie, that orangy weed hardy enough to sprout near the railroad tracks up and down the Eastern seaboard. The moss lining hiding the container can be seen through the slats of the twig box; on the table, a cushion of yellow wildflowers in a small 19th-century Chinese pot.

B. A bit of fancy breathes life into a functional — and very personal — room. This nosegay, for instance, of miniature glads, roses, lilies, and Queen Anne's lace, perches on a ledge of the bathroom cupboard.

80

My copper mold is overflowing with sweet-smelling basil, grassy chives, and cornflowers (also called bluebonnets and bachelor's buttons). My old cruet holds sprigs of dill.

Herbs

Anything green that grew out of the mold was an excellent herb to our fathers of old.

— Rudyard Kipling

If asked to name one room in a house that means home most of us would say the kitchen, where we pass so many of our waking hours. I love to keep casually arranged flowers and herbs on the kitchen counter. Not only do potted and cut herbs look pretty and smell wonderful, they taste good. And how convenient to have fresh ones on hand for salads and sauces. Fill a jam pot with parsley, thyme, or mint. Set it next to a bowl of pansies and should you tire of the mundane, garnish your soup with pansy leaves, as they did years ago. Or for a bit of pretension so esoteric only you will know, toss nasturtium leaves in a Fourth of July salad. The nasturtium happens to symbolize patriotism.

Many herbs can be grown on the kitchen windowsill, for example chives, marjoram, basil, sage, parsley, thyme, winter savory, and rosemary — one of the most fragrant herbs and the easiest to grow indoors. Herbs are seed plants and annuals, with soft green stems that wither after each season's growth. Woody-stemmed plants, on the other hand, are perennials. Herbs thrive in cool sunny spots, and in rich well-drained soil. Indeed they are so generous they will even produce in poor soil. Keep them away from drafts, and water them frequently. In dry climates, create a more humid atmosphere by standing herb pots on a bed of wet gravel.

Should you have an outdoors, an herb garden is splendid. Remember to position the taller herbs on the side of the garden so they do not overshadow the smaller ones. And if you plant tarragon and mint, put them in pots first and then sink the pots in the soil. If you do not take this precaution, you could find their roots overrunning the entire garden. Basil, dill, and parsley can be started outside, and moved into the kitchen during the cooler months.

We think of herbs as seasonings only, but an herb is also any plant used medicinally. Before the development of modern drugs, plants and flowers were the main source of medication. Countless remedies for all manner of ailments were brewed from flowers we now think of as merely decorative: chrysanthemums, cornflowers, roses, snapdragons — to name a few. One early herb manual suggests a woman restore youth by daily cleansings with water in which snapdragon seeds had steeped.

By the way, dried herbs, which keep their fragrance for some time in the open air and seemingly forever in a tightly closed jar, are often used as a base for potpourri.

Daisies

*To see this flower against
the sunny spread
When it
riseth early by the morrow,
That blissful sight softeneth
all my sorrow.*

— Chaucer

The French named it *la marguerite*; in Old English it was "herb margaret." To the Scots it is the gowan; in Yorkshire it is the bairnwort, or flower beloved by children. To farmers, it is a weed.

If there is any other flower so universal in its appeal as the daisy, it is a secret well kept. Quite literally it means *day's eye*, an apt description for this yellow-centered blossom with its innocent and sprightly cast.

A daisy plant is an ideal indoor decoration, which holds up well for weeks. In the garden it blooms throughout the summer in a cool sunny spot, and can be cut back after flowering to ensure blooms in the fall. Try growing your own daisy plant by rooting the side shoots of a cut daisy.

Daisies are high on my personal list of favorite flowers. What could be more like spring (they are actually grown year-round) than a big basket of fresh daisies? And as if daisies were not endowed with enough charms, they are also sturdy and inexpensive. However, certain demands have to be met if daisies are to be healthy.

First, they must be almost totally defoliated. If not, their leaves will drain the water, causing the flower heads to wilt after only a day or two. Next, always cut with a knife; their cells tend to dry out and close up more rapidly than those of many other flowers. Alas, nothing is without flaws. Roses and daisies discharge so much bacteria that it is a good idea to add a bacteria retardant to the water. And a flower nutrient cannot hurt.

After several days the bottom two or three inches of the daisy stem may have rotted to the point where the flower can no longer draw water. (Daisies draw water through the outside of the stem, while some flowers draw it only through the base of the stem.) When the lower portion rots, make a new cut to expose fresh water-conducting cells. Daisies are generous by nature, and will repay three-fold the small amount of extra attention given them.

Daisy Fishbowl

Simplicity is seldom a mistake. Daisies in a round, clear glass bowl — a fishbowl as it is commonly known — look grand.

This is how to construct an arrangement in a fishbowl. I used daisies, but you may substitute any firm-stemmed flower, or a mix of flowers.

After conditioning the daisies, strip off most of their foliage.

Fill the fishbowl half full with lukewarm water. I find an eight- to ten-inch bowl works well with marguerite daisies.

Cut and scrape the stem of the first daisy and lay its head on the rim of one side of the bowl, slanting it down so the stem is in water. Brace the base of its stem on the opposite side of the container. Lay more daisies — cutting each as you do so — around the entire rim, and brace them in the same fashion. You now have a web of stems to serve as your arranging mesh. (Number 1 in the illustration.)

Finish the arrangement (remembering to put the first daisy in the center) by standing, and angling, the rest of the flowers in the bowl. All will be held in place by the webbing created by the stems. (Number 2 in the illustration.)

For an arrangement with a somewhat round shape, some of the center daisies should be tall, as should a few used at the base. (Number 3 in the illustration.)

Daisies in a bowl can go just about anywhere at any time. They are indeed "daisy," which in old slang means something choice or excellent.

Constructing an arrangement is much like painting a picture or creating a fine meal. It is a building process comprising several steps.

Opposite: Marguerite daisies perfectly complement this blue and white library. The cheery and happy-looking daisy is inexpensive as well as easily found.

Appendix

Here are some general rules for conditioning:
Cut thin stems on the diagonal with a knife.
Break woody stems and split ends.
Place flower stems and branches in a bucket of deep cool water for an hour or more before arranging. Be sure not to crowd them. Some flowers benefit from having their stems plunged in boiling water for a few minutes before standing in cool water, which prevents juices from escaping the stems, hastens bud development, and revives wilted flowers.

Common Name	Botanical Name	Traditional Meaning	When to Cut or Buy	Color	Estimated Lifespan in Water	Useful Comments
Agapanthus (African lily)	*Agapanthus africanus*	Love	In full bloom.	Blue violet Cream	One week.	Condition by removing lower foliage, and place in deep cool water. Preserve by hanging seed heads down.
Allium (Ornamental onion)	*Allium giganteum*		In full bloom.	Blue violet	One week.	Condition in cool water. To remove onion odor, add one teaspoon of bleach to full vase of water.
Alstroemeria (Peruvian lily)	*Alstroemeria aurantiaca* *Alstroemeria Ligtu*		When slightly open.	White Pink Mauve Yellow Coral	One to two weeks.	Cut stem and place in cool water. The delicate trumpet-shaped flower is lovely to use in mixed arrangements.

Common Name	Botanical Name	Traditional Meaning	When to Cut or Buy	Color	Estimated Lifespan in Water	Useful Comments
Anemone (Windflower)	*Anemone coronaria*	Sickness	In somewhat tight stage.	Pink Red Blue Purple White with dark centers	Five to seven days.	Anemones do not draw water well from green foam. Keep cool. Add more water on second day. Anemones look well used en masse. A single flower is perfect for a bud vase with one galax leaf.
Aster	*Callistephus chinensis*	Variety	In full bloom.	White Pink Rose Lavender Purple (No Yellow.)	Seven to ten days.	Condition for several hours before arranging. Wire, as heads may tip and cut off water supply. Remove lower leaves. Scrape and break woody stems or hammer them. Asters last better if boiling water method is used.
Baby's Breath (Chalk plant)	*Gypsophila paniculata*		In full bloom.	White Pink	One week.	Condition in cool water one hour before arranging. Dries easily by hanging, or standing in water until water evaporates. (Flowers shrink as they dry and turn beige.)
Bachelor's Button (Corn flower)	*Centaurea Cyanus*	Single blessed-ness	In full bloom, and when color is rich.	Royal blue (Purple, Pink, White, are less common.)	One week.	Cut off dead shoots to promote more bloom. Condition in deep water. Color fades as flower ages.
Carnation	*Dianthus caryophyllus*	Fascination Striped: Refusal Yellow: Disdain	In full bloom. Head should feel firm.	White Yellow Pink Red Mauve Bicolors	Seven to ten days.	If underdeveloped, condition in hot water; otherwise condition in lukewarm water. Cut on the slant just above a stem joint. Remove bottom leaves. Carnations last better arranged by themselves, but look well used many different ways.

Common Name	Botanical Name	Traditional Meaning	When to Cut or Buy	Color	Estimated Lifespan in Water	Useful Comments
Chrysanthe-mum (Shasta daisy, Mums, Pompons, Spider mums, Daisy poms)	*Chrysanthemum morifolium*	Red: Love Yellow: Slighted love White: Truth	In full bloom. Centers should not have brown edges.	Various (No blue.)	Two weeks.	Break stems, scrape and split ends with knife. Remove most of foliage, as it wilts many days before flower fades. Condition by standing in deep cool water one hour or more before arranging. Avoid buying cut or potted mums and poms when buds are tight and not showing color. They might refuse to develop.
Daffodil	*Narcissus*	Regard Great yellow: Chivalry	In bud stage with some color showing.	Yellow White Orange Bicolors	Two to three days. (Greenhouse daffs last up to a week.)	Wipe off oozing sap before putting in water. Condition in shallow water one hour before arranging. Condition foliage separately.
Dahlia	*Dahlia variabilis*	Good taste Instability	In bloom. When buying, be sure petals are crisp.	Various (No pure blue.)	Five days.	Cut the hollow stems on the diagonal and slit them vertically to increase water flow. To prevent juice from escaping the stems, condition in boiling water for a few minutes before placing in cool water for one hour. To make them last longer, add a little sugar to water before arranging. Some say aspirin also helps.
Daisy (Marguerite)	*Chrysanthemum frutescens*	Innocence	In full bloom. Buy when petals face upwards.	White Yellow with yellow centers	Ten days.	Be sure to remove most of the foliage. With a knife, cut and scrape base of stem. Use flower food in water to retard bacteria formation. Dip daisy stems (once cut) in boiling water, then leave up to their necks in deep water.

Common Name	Botanical Name	Traditional Meaning	When to Cut or Buy	Color	Estimated Lifespan in Water	Useful Comments
Delphinium	*Delphinium hybridum*		When half of flowers on stalk are open.	Blue Purple White Pink Mauve	One week.	Delphinium sheds when fading. Make vertical slit in hollow stem to increase water flow. Cut base diagonally with knife. Try conditioning by turning upside down and filling hollow stems with water. Plug ends with a bit of lamb's wool. Generally, just give stems a long drink in deep water before arranging. Change water often.
Dogwood	*Cornus florida*	Durability	In bud, showing color.	White Pink Yellow	Five to seven days.	Break and hammer stem. Peel two inches of bark from stem and split stems. Soak in deep cool water for 12 hours before arranging.
Freesia	*Freesia refracta* *Freesia hybrida*		When top bloom is in bud but showing color.	Yellow White Mauve Blue Pink Red Magenta	Five days.	Cut stems with knife. Give a long drink before arranging. Remove individual blooms after they wither. Beautiful scent.
Gladiolus	*Gladiolus*	Strength of character Pain and tears	When blossoms are starting to show color.	Yellow White Purple Orange Red	Up to two weeks.	Cut stems under running water. Recut in a few days. Break off thin top to encourage all blooms to open. Condition in shallow cool water for half a day before arranging. Snap off withered florets from time to time. Change water.
Gerbera (African daisy or Transvaal daisy)	*Gerbera Jamesonii*		In full bloom and when petals face upwards.	Various (No blue.)	Four to five days.	Perfect, almost artificial-looking blossoms. Flowers usually need wiring to support heavy heads. Place ends of stems in boiling water before giving a long drink in deep cool water. Wonderful in mixed arrangements or as decoration on a food platter.

Common Name	Botanical Name	Traditional Meaning	When to Cut or Buy	Color	Estimated Lifespan in Water	Useful Comments
Hyacinth	*Hyacinthus orientalis*	Sport Game Play Purple: Sorrow Blue: Constancy White: Unobtrusive loveliness	When buds at top of stalks are tight.	White Cream Blue Purple Pink Rose	Several days.	Wipe sap from stem ends. Condition and arrange in shallow water. Recut stems daily and add fresh water. Condition grape hyacinth in water in refrigerator for an hour before arranging. Hardy.
Hydrangea	*Hydrangea macrophylla* *Hydrangea paniculata*	A boaster Heartless-ness	In full bloom.	Green Cream Pink Mauve Blue Red	One week. (After a few days will begin to dry in arrangement.)	Break and split stems, cutting upward for one inch. Scrape bottom part of stems. Heavy drinkers. Stand branches in buckets of water in dark room for several hours before arranging. To dry: let dry on shrub or by standing in water which eventually evaporates. Air drying causes blossoms to lose color and turn brown.
Iris	*Iris*	Message German Iris: Flame	In bud stage or on the break.	White Yellow Blue Purple Orange Pink Red	A few days only.	Remove and cut ends of foliage. Condition separately. Stand flower stalks in shallow cool water one hour or more before arranging.
Lilac	*Syringa vulgaris*	Field: Humility Purple: First emotions of love White: Youthful innocence	In full bloom.	Purple White French lilac: White Purple Pink Blue	A few days to one week.	To condition: 1. Remove most of foliage. Peel bark up two inches at stem base. Cut stems crosswise. Hammer stem. OR: 2. Submerge complete branch, blossom, and stem in deep cool water overnight before arranging. (This works for hydrangeas, too.) Hammer stems. Heavenly scent.
Lily	*Lilium*	Day: Coquetry Yellow: Falsehood Gaiety	In bud form, showing color. When petals are curled backward, blossoms are fading.	All colors except blue.	Ten to fourteen days.	Cut ends of stems on the slant and give long drink in deep cold water. Do not force in hot water or stems will weaken. Remove most of foliage as it fades and turns yellow before blossom wilts. Loose pollen can be messy. Many species have wonderful scents.

Common Name	Botanical Name	Traditional Meaning	When to Cut or Buy	Color	Estimated Lifespan in Water	Useful Comments
Lily of the Valley	*Convallaria majalis*	Return of happiness	In bud or full blossom. When buying, top buds should be closed.	White	A few days.	If "pulled" from the garden, cut with knife and place in water one hour before arranging. Greenhouse blooms should be wrapped in tissue and put in shallow warm water; after an hour add more water and let stand overnight in deep water. Arrange in shallow water the next day. Some experts stand stalks in water in refrigerator for an hour before arranging, eliminating overnight conditioning.
Marigold	*Tagetes*	Grief Despair French: Jealousy	In full bloom or in bud. Centers should be tight.	Yellow Gold Orange Rust Bicolors	One week or more.	Cut, remove bottom foliage. Let stand up to their necks in cool water for one hour before arranging. Foliage has pungent odor, making marigolds unpopular for use in dinner table arrangements.
Paper-White Narcissus	*Narcissus Tazetta*	Egotism	In bud or just open.	White	A few days.	Cut ½ inch off bottom; stand in deep cool water for an hour or more before arranging in shallow water. Lovely scent.
Orchid	*Cattleya Cymbidium hybrids Cypripedium reginae Dendrobium nobile Odontoglossum hybrids Oncidium Phalaenopsis Vanda hybrida*	A belle	In full bloom.	Blue Yellow White Rose Purple Brown Red	Up to two-and a-half weeks depending on variety.	There are over 500 genera in this big family of long-lasting flowers. Cut stems on a slant and give flowers a good drink. Remove from water; recut ends of stems before replacing in fresh water. The lacy branch orchids are less hardy than the larger-headed blooms.

Common Name	Botanical Name	Traditional Meaning	When to Cut or Buy	Color	Estimated Lifespan in Water	Useful Comments
Peony	*Paeonia*	Shame Bashful-ness	In bud form. Blooms open in a few hours after cutting and placing in water.	White Pale pink Yellow Rose Magenta (called red)	Five to eight days.	Cut with knife. Remove all foliage below waterline. Warm to hot water can be used for forcing open the flower. Cut and slit ends of stems. Plunge stalks in deep cool water for a few hours before arranging. Condition leaves separately. They look well mixed with other flowers.
Queen Anne's lace (Wild carrot)	*Daucus Carota*		When necks are sturdy and there is no shedding.	Off-white	Seven to ten days.	Cut with knife. Condition in deep cool water up to necks. Singe stem ends to prevent shedding as flower fades. Greenhouse varieties are more fragile than field-house types.
Ranunculus (Buttercup)	*Ranunculus asiaticus*	You are radiant with charms.	In full bloom. Be certain stems have no mold and leaves are not yellow.	Yellow Orange White Rose Red	Several days.	Put ends of stems in boiling water for a few minutes before giving a long drink of cool water for at least one hour.
Rose	*Rosa*	Love	In bud form or in a somewhat developed stage.	Red Pink Ivory White Lavender Coral Gold Lemon Orange	A few days to two weeks.	Remove bottom thorns and leaves. Cut stems on the diagonal with a sharp knife. Plunge in cool water in a cool room (or refrigerator) overnight before arranging. Recut and change water often. Use flower food to retard bacteria growth. To revive tipped heads, put stem ends in boiling water before the conditioning process. Magnificent fragrance.
Snapdragon	*Antirrhinum majus*		Cut when lower flowers are open. Buy in full bloom, with top flowers in bud stage.	White Yellow Orange Pink Magenta Purple	Up to one week or more.	Remove bottom foliage. Cut stems under water to revive blossoms. Plunge stalks in deep warm water for one hour or more before arranging. (Greenhouse snaps may benefit from the boiling water treatment.)

Common Name	Botanical Name	Traditional Meaning	When to Cut or Buy	Color	Estimated Lifespan in Water	Useful Comments
Star of Bethlehem (Chincherinchee)	*Ornithogalum umbellatum* *Ornithogalum thyrsoides*	Purity	In bud form with some color showing.	White with green Cream	Three weeks or more.	Condition by cutting with sharp cut. Remove flowers as they wither. Change water often. Cut stems after five days or so. Tight green crown can be broken off to give flower a less exotic and softer look.
Sweet William (Pinks)	*Dianthus barbatus*	Gallantry	Cut in full bloom. Buy when flowers have only a few withered buds.	Rose White Magenta Pink Coral Purple	One week or more.	Condition by cutting just above stem joint and plunging in deep cool water for an hour or so. Blossoms look well clustered together.
Tuberose	*Polianthes tuberosa*	Dangerous pleasures	In full bloom.	White Cream	One week.	Pull off withered blooms as they fade. Condition by cutting stems and plunging in deep cool water for one hour before arranging. Beautiful fragrance.
Tulip	*Tulipa*	Red: Declaration of love Variegated: Beautiful eyes Yellow: Hopeless love	In bud form, showing some color.	Various Bicolors	Five to eight days.	Cut one inch off bottom of stems and remove some of the foliage. Wrap blossoms in tube of non-absorbent paper; stand tube in deep water for a few hours. Tulips should be straight. Condition foliage separately. Recut stems and add fresh water often. Stick pin through stem just under flower head and tulips will last longer. A teaspoon of sugar in flower water works well.
Zinnia	*Zinnia elegans*	Thoughts of absent friends.	Buy in full bloom. Cut in full bloom or when buds are ready to open.	Various Bicolors (Not blue.)	Up to one week or more.	Remove bottom foliage and side shoots. Condition in boiling water for a few minutes and then in deep cool water for one hour or more before arranging.

Acknowledgments

I am indebted to Beverly Kempton, my friend and editor, for her encouragement, her dedication to the scholarship of the subject, and her fine sense of when to use the right word at the right time.

Then too, I am sincerely grateful to Jerry Markell and Axel Behnke of Mutual Cut Flower Co., Inc. for their valuable assistance over the years, and to my friend Elvin McDonald, the noted writer and lecturer on plants, for the loan of his fine photographs and his valuable advice.

A special thank you to Frank Kelly, a fine floral designer; to Betsy and Larry Blau; and Pierre and Gabor Saint-Denis, owners of Le Refuge, who permitted full use of their restaurant for several photographs. And my gratitude to Everett Fahy, Director of The Frick Collection and a knowledgeable gardener, for his guidance on the appendix.

Many others have helped to make this book possible, and I am lastingly appreciative of assistance from: Martha Hoffmann, my business associate; Tom Dooley; Clare and Jack Fraser; Greg Komar; Brian Leahy; Michael Lutin; Christopher Blau; the staff of Mutual Cut Flower; Chingos and Sons, Inc.; Charles Russell, of Bouquets a la Carte; Jeanne Cameron Shanks; Bertha Brown Unger, who contributed instructions for the succulent wreath; Cathy and Al Possehl for their advice on bulb plants; and the staff of the Library of The New York Botanical Gardens.

Lastly, I would like to dedicate this book to my husband Jim, and my parents Irma and Charles Farran, all of whom gave such endless support and encouragement.

Index